JEKYLL AND ME NOT

By Sherry Bach

Introduction
By
Pierre J. Samaan, Ph.D.

"No man, for any considerable period, can wear one face to himself, and another to the multitude without finally getting bewildered as to which may be the true."

Nathaniel Hawthorne
Scarlet Letter [1]

Disclaimer and note from the Author:

Jekyll and Hide Me Not is based on a true story. Names, dates and details of events have been changed to protect the innocent. "Based on a true story" means that the author has taken truth and applied fiction liberties intertwined in and around that truth. To delineate which events are true and which events are not true would be to totally miss the point of *Jekyll and Hide Me Not* and the author refuses to do so. The author's purpose for writing *Jekyll and Hide Me Not* is to help other women, through a fiction work, to recognize behavior in men who have the potential to be abusive: emotionally, mentally, physically or verbally. The author is not licensed in any way as a mental health professional and the thoughts here within are solely based on the author's personal experience and opinions, as well as five years of research on the subject of Narcissistic Personality Disorder. Reference material is noted where applicable.

INTRODUCTION
By Pierre J. Samaan, Ph.D.

As a Clinical Pastoral Counselor, I can relate very well to what Sherry Bach has written. The relational situations in this book are true to life. I see the same difficult circumstances painfully exposed on a daily basis in my Christian Counseling office. Ms. Bach has effectively depicted in one woman's life pieces of the lives of many women who feel trapped in the bondage of an abusive or unhappy marriage and life pattern.

These are conflicted marriages where a partner, usually alone in his or her efforts, is striving to meet Biblical standards of love and forgiveness within the vows of the marriage. Christian couples have a higher standard to follow than does a secular couple. After all, in our culture today, the institution of marriage is being undermined by those who do not have to hold to a morally high Biblical standard.

What does a person of high values and morals do when, believing he or she has made an excellent decision to marry someone, later learning that he or she has made a mistake? In the secular world it is easy, divorce and try again; or just live together with the next one. However, for those of us who have committed our lives to a higher standard, we must struggle through spiritual warfare to come to a place in our lives that God has created, serenity.

Unfortunately, we are living in a growing culture of entitlement. More and more people are feeling like they are deserving of certain privileges, even though they have not earned the right to obtain these privileges. An increasing number of these individuals have developed an exaggerated belief that they deserve special treatment, admiration, and ideal love.

Most people work hard to achieve what they have. However, the chronic taker or emotional thief must steal what he has never learned to attain on his own merit. Others are telling him that he is wrong to emotionally rob and abuse his victim. Since he has not earned the right to these life privileges, he must justify in his own mind why it is alright to emotionally steal from and destroy family or friends.

The secular world, in psychology, has a title for the more severe interpersonally exploitive persons, *Narcissistic Personality Disorder* (NPD). In Clinical Pastoral Counseling we will also use a term to describe an NPD as one who has a *Jezebel spirit* (1 Kings 16:31 – 2 Kings 9:37). In the Bible, Jezebel was a rebellious person who latched onto Ahab, the King of Judah, by marriage. Because of her manipulations, pride, and self-promotion, she caused the destruction of Judah, Israel's northern kingdom. The man or woman with NPD, like the Jezebel spirit, will begin forming early in life and leave a trail of damage throughout his or her life if unchanged.

It is true that most youth go through a narcissistic phase in adolescence that they will eventually outgrow. While some may remain puffed-up in their narcissistic love for themselves, the more severe will develop an exploitive skill that leads to a lack of both

4

empathy and conscience. They have finally earned a title of their own, NPD.

In her book, Jekyll and Hyde Me Not, Sherry Bach has laid out before the reader a dramatic encounter of a spiritually devoted wife battling the painful embraces of a husband with NPD. Uniquely, Ms. Bach has the wife, Alexis, see her situation through a life parallel (for you to read about) to help her better understand her seemingly powerless situation.

I hope that as you read this book you too will begin to find life parallels to help you better understand your life situation and God's special plan for you.

Pierre J. Samaan, Ph.D.

CHAPTER ONE

"As an atheist for thirty-one years, you could hardly say that I, Alexis Cole, was lukewarm toward God, as are some individuals who claim to be living for the King. However, if you followed them out on a Friday night, you would learn otherwise. No, I was exceedingly cold regarding the entire subject of our creator and did not masquerade to the contrary. I knew I was not living for anyone but me; my wants, my needs. Everyone who had ever approached the subject of God with me was aware of this fact. Still, according to worldly terms, I was considered a goody-two-shoes in some arenas because as an adult I did not smoke, only drank occasionally, did not do drugs, or cuss and tried to maintain good physical condition.

I started smoking cigarettes at age twelve which were given to me by my mother's husband; we will call him Ivan. I smoked for a few years but had given them up around the age of sixteen. At eleven, Ivan's children, who were older than me, gave me marijuana to smoke, which I gave up by age fourteen. From fourteen to seventeen I drank alcohol off and on with the worst age of this season being fourteen due to the kids I hung out with from school; we moved before I was very ingrained in it…"

The speaker was certainly holding the attention of the audience, partly from shock value, and especially considering the truth and bluntness with which she spoke. There was an obvious contradiction between her childhood and her present life. Those in attendance were mainly high school age Christians, who had gathered for a youth event at a church in North Florida.

Ms. Cole went on to explain the course of events that would eventually bring her to belief in God, leaving out the explicit details that she thought were inappropriate for teenagers. This explication included a friend who never gave up on her, Christian radio, hell fire and brimstone preaching, and the bottom of the pit she found herself lying in, figuratively speaking, when her husband left her. For a split second she wanted to be dead, especially upon learning that her lover was not going to leave his wife for her. It was at that moment in her life, she elucidated to the audience, that she felt enough pain to want to stop that pain.

The fleeting thought of wanting to be dead only lasted a brief moment and was a wake up call for her bringing to front and center the direction she had taken, the bad decisions she had made. She did not recognize the emotion as a suicidal tendency, but just a meaningless "I wish I was dead". It was so transient that it disappeared almost as soon as it came washed away by the thought of her children. However, years later Alexis wondered what seed from that thought might have germinated had it not been for her kids. Would it have turned suicidal she asked herself.

The level of emotional pain she felt at the bottom of the pit created the unrelenting desire to turn the vehicle she was driving around, point it in the right direction and begin seeking the right road diligently. The pain of untruths will keep coming until they are stopped with reality she told her audience.

With that genuine change of heart, which her now "ex-husband" would criticize as insincere and a fad, God would allow a chain of events, called his providence, to unravel in her life, bridging the gap between the unsaved soul and eternity with God. She found a Bible believing church and was immersed into Christ after her confession of faith, re-enacting the death, burial, and resurrection of her Savior as she rose to walk in newness of life, being promised the gift of the indwelling Holy Spirit. She would pass from darkness into light at the age of thirty-one, her children age two and five at the time, and find peace and joy with God, knowing that she had been forgiven of every sin she ever committed.

Alexis wished she had more than one hour with these teens to intimately discuss the details of the ten years following her conversion from atheism to Christianity in hopes of preparing them, equipping them for the fight between good and evil; this was an area she felt the church was negligent in: teaching their members how to battle the enemy. An intelligent commanding officer would not send an army battalion into battle without proper equipment, and the church certainly should not send Christians into the world without making it clear to them they need armor for the impending war against demonic activity.

Some of the teens in attendance had been taught that demons did not exist today. They were taught that the demons were bound up and deemed impotent at the crucifixion; Alexis knew otherwise. She thought about one of her favorite quotes and relayed it to the teens; it was by Ulysses S. Grant[2] who spoke about the Civil war at the time but she found it very appropriate for spiritual warfare today. He said, "The art of war is simple enough. Find out where your enemy is. Get at him as soon as you can. Strike at him as hard as you can and as often as you can and keep moving on." Satan and his helpers were certainly enemies of the church and one of their most effective tools was to make believers think they were powerless to affect their lives.

Speaking about it always caused the particulars of her early Christian walk to play on the big screen in her head and tonight was no exception as she drove back to her hotel room after the speaking engagement later that evening.

She would always remember the night of, and day after, her baptism. She went to work feeling like a new person and could not wait to tell someone as she approached her desk. The other secretary smiled at her, not quite sure what to say other than, "That's great", when she reported that she had been saved last night.

Alexis recapitulated in her mind the eight months following her conversion, which were spent with enthusiasm and excitement for God as she tried to convince her ex-lover that what they had done was wrong, and convince her family that they needed to seek God. Her ex-lover finally told her that if all she was going to do was talk about God, he would rather not hear from her. The family was losing their patience with her as well. Alexis was starting to see life differently, see people differently, especially Ivan, her mother's husband.

Ivan listened one day at lunch as one of Alexis' friends spoke about the Bible and what it taught. Alexis was going to save the world that first year she became a Christian and Ivan was top on the list. But his reaction to the discussion was nothing less than contemptible. He denounced the teachings demanding he knew better becoming angry anyone would suggest otherwise or disagree with him. His reaction to her outreach really surprised Alexis who most of her life thought of Ivan as intelligent and fun loving. She never viewed him as evil, but reality began to be revealed under the light and microscope of truth and slowly Ivan started to look wicked, in word, in thought and in deed. He had buffaloed her until the light revealed who he really was.

It was after this luncheon that Ivan would team up with her ex-husband secretly to try to "destroy her", Ivan's words exactly. She had been a Christian approximately one year and this person was someone she had known as her stepfather since she was nine and now he was trying to destroy her. How could that be? Confusion tried to alter what she knew but the truth filtered it making his intentions very clear to the point where she did not hesitate in severing their relationship altogether.

The destruction team came up with their first plan and it included the children. Alexis had received papers in the mail claiming that her kids were in immediate danger, because of her religion, and should be taken away from her and given to her ex-husband…his idea of course. The document went so far as to say Alexis had become a member of a cult. She took the papers to a

10

consultation with an attorney who advised her that she had ten days to respond to the accusations, however, her ex-husband had sent the document through the mail instead of serving her in person as dictated by law. Eight of her ten day response time had lapsed.

So one night as Alexis was coming home from work, three sheriffs pulled up in their cars and pulled Alexis' children out of her arms as they were crying; the children were two and five at the time. Alexis was screaming, "How could this happen? I just received papers yesterday." The sheriff allowed the children and Alexis to go up to her apartment to get some stuff for the kids; her two year old daughter wanted her "blankie." Alexis was hysterical and just kept asking the sheriff over and over how this could happen. For the first time in her Christian walk, she experienced the feeling of wanting to tear her clothes because of grief as the Bible described in some of its history. She threw herself on the floor sobbing with emotional pain as the squad car drove away with the children. Alexis called a friend who was by her side in five minutes. That night Alexis met with the elders at her church who retained an attorney for her; he did pro bono work.

The father of the children who was licensed as a lawyer in another state had plans to leave with the children as soon as possible with Ivan's help. The documents they had filed were illegal, first of all because, the father was claiming he lived in the state where he was licensed as a lawyer when he had not lived there in almost two years. Secondly, instead of serving Alexis with the papers through the courts where they were both residents, he had filed them in

11

another state and sent them to her through the mail. It was an incredible tangled web of confusion. The lawyer that would represent Alexis in the case begged her to have her ex disbarred for the illegal filings but for whatever reason she did not pursue it because she felt like it would be returning evil for evil which she believed was the wrong thing to do.

The next day at her work, Alexis was served papers to show up to an emergency hearing at the court house. She was shaking with terror. Alexis was not sure why the emergency hearing had been called, and would never find out, however, she suspected that the sheriff who had gone into her apartment with her to get the kids' things, tipped off the judge or someone about the situation. Alexis' apartment was clean and orderly and the kids had a nice room, filled with various stuffed animals, kid posters, lots of books, and toys. It was hardly an environment that gave the appearance of "immediate danger".

After the four-hour emergency hearing called by the Judge himself, whereby Alexis defended her religious beliefs on the stand in the courtroom, the kids went home with her that night and the first collusion begun by her ex and Ivan would be unsuccessful. She could not believe in the twenty first century in America, she was on the stand answering questions under oath about what religious doctrine she followed, which was the Bible, and the Bible only. She knew she had not been a perfect wife as an atheist, but the sins she had committed were morally wrong, not illegal. The whole thing bore resemblance to the Salem witch trials.

Interrogation on the stand regarding her childhood forced her to answer questions about how Ivan had given her pornographic magazines and stuck his tongue in her mouth once when she was fourteen, and often said inappropriate things to her when she was a teenager like her butt looked sexy.

The outcome of the whole thing was amazing to her as she watched this show on her mind's screen and how the people who were attacking her, became their own target and God worked it all out for good during a time when Alexis felt totally helpless and powerless to do anything but pray. She remembered how she meditated on the scripture out of Deuteronomy that says, "The Lord will cause your enemies who rise against thee, to be defeated before your face; they shall come out against you one way, and flee before you seven ways."

She began to notice a look about Ivan's eyes; the look was very evil and perverse. His eyes had always looked that way, but Alexis did not recognize them as evil, but now as she viewed old photos to throw out she could see it. It was almost like God was revealing to her the look of evil. Alexis was a strong believer in the delineation between good and evil and knew that scripture says the eyes are a light unto the soul. This was when a memory was invoked in her data bank.

When she was nineteen she dated a man who brought her to a church in Kansas City, Kansas once or twice. Alexis was not ready for faith at that time and considered herself an atheist, however, she remembered noticing several people who seemed to have their faces illuminated. It was beautiful. She could not stop staring at these people who had this beautiful look and it made an impression on her; she had never seen anything like it before. She never mentioned it to anyone until after she became a Christian. What was she going to say to her friends back then, "The people looked like they had light bulbs in their heads"? They would have laughed at her. Besides, she did not really understand exactly what she was seeing, only that it appeared to be a light of some sort. Now she was also noticing an opposite look on faces and in eyes; it was not an illumination but a revealing of the absence of light…darkness. Alexis had always been attracted to light whether it was the stars in the dark sky, bulbs on a Christmas tree, flame from a camp fire, or fireworks.

Ivan read the court transcripts and abhorred the fact that he was exposed for what he really was even though he denied it all and would continue to deny it to his grave. He continued his ploy to destroy along with Alexis' ex, even after the first defeat in court. For their second destruction attempt they assembled packets together laden with lies, and sent them to Alexis' place of employment, and the church. Ivan told her he would destroy her at her job, in the church and in the community; that was their plan.

This strategy never succeeded and nothing ever became of any of it except the packets were returned to Alexis. The Lord continued to bless and protect her and the children as the ex-husband eventually retreated for two years back to the state he falsely claimed he lived in. Ivan died a few years later.

As a new Christian, Alexis benefited from the promises of God and was rewarded for her obedience and faithfulness to His word through these first few years of her Christian walk. She had begun right away reading the Bible front to back and was very sober about her faith; however, at the time of the court event she was yet ignorant of the propensity some people have for evil, and the seriousness of Satan's mission.

The scripture that states Satan is roaming the earth looking for whom he can devour, trying to kill, steal, and destroy was beginning to make application to real life for Alexis. How did Satan accomplish his work though? She was curious. If a third of the angels choose to reside with Satan, does that mean he uses them to execute his plan of destruction? How? Do they have access to our minds? Can they afflict us; deceive us? Does God counter their deception with truth? How do we beat Satan when he seems so powerful and continual?

The reality of the answers to these questions was forthcoming for Alexis although she had an incline that she had ticked Satan off; she could feel it, it was almost tangible. As an atheist, she was not a threat to him; as a Christian she was a serious threat because she was somber about being a Christian. Her mother always told her, if you are going to do something, do it right or don't do it at all, and this was exactly how Alexis approached living as a believer; it did not make sense to her any other way.

The memories continued to flow as she drove and even after she arrived at her hotel. She focused on the amazement of the

15

brain's capacity to remember and play back situations at mach speed with prodigious detail. For whatever odd reason, she thought about how weird it was that just thinking of biting into a lemon the way she would an apple made the glands in her mouth burst in response to the sourness, even though she was not actually doing it, bringing alive the scripture that says, as a man thinks in his heart, so is he.

The next thought jumped to a comparison between, her current spiritual maturity, and where she was back when the emergency court hearing was called ten years ago. It had been a painful growth but somehow had joy in it. What a contradiction: "painful joy"; a parallel depicting pregnancy and childbirth to spiritual growth. Sometimes it was painful as her uterus and stomach stretched to capacity but the joy found in feeling the baby move and holding a new life in her arms once the pregnancy was over was more than she could have ever dreamed possible, overshadowing the pain; the same relief she felt when the in and out of court activity caused by her ex husband finally ceased for good which was an answer to one of her prayers.

While she was taking a shower and preparing for bed, Alexis continued to play the "Ten Years After Conversion" movie in her mind, praying every other minute thanking God for saving her and delivering her from the evil conspired against her.

After the court victory, life was good for awhile, until an older man from the church befriended Alexis and her kids. He would bring over the two-for-one specials from the grocery store, give them a tree at Christmas time; he even took the whole family to

Disney twice. Superficially, it all appeared to be commendable on his part and good for Alexis as a single mom; he was a widower.

Alexis never left the children alone with him except once when he took her five-year-old daughter without her to a state springs known for its scenic boat rides. Prior to this, she had been gathering red flagged data about this man that made her cautious; subtle flags that most people probably would have never noticed or given much credence to: the jewelry he bought her daughter, the fact that he called her daughter "lover" and she was five years old, paying more attention to her daughter than her son, and a picture in his home that he had taken of his grade school aged granddaughter posed in a one piece swimsuit like a pin up girl.

Alexis had heard from the surgeon general that you should start sex education with children when they are three years old, appropriate for their age level of course, and that was exactly what she had done. Therefore, her daughter knew at age five that no one was suppose to kiss her on the lips or touch her private parts. When her daughter returned from the trip to the springs and reported that the man wanted to kiss her on the lips, Alexis tried to stay calm, asking, "What did you say to him?" All the while wanting to scream out loud. Her daughter responded, "I told him that my mommy says that no one kisses me on the lips."

"What did he say?"
"He said, your mommy's not here."
"What did you do?" Alexis could feel the warmth of anger competing with the fire of fear to see which one could reach her face first.

"I turned my cheek."

Alexis was relieved but further probed her daughter with questions to make sure nothing had happened. Even though Alexis was confident her daughter told her everything and it seemed no harm was done, after this incident, she severed that relationship in spite of the fact that some people in the church defended the man. Approximately three years after this incident with Alexis' daughter, the man was convicted of sexual intercourse with his eight-year-old granddaughter and sentenced to fifteen years in prison. "That would have been my daughter" Alexis dramatized as she thanked God for his protection once again out loud in the hotel shower while shaving her legs.

Alexis remained single for seven years after her divorce focusing primarily on raising her kids. She briefly tried dating but soon learned it was not going to work for her or be beneficial to the children, so she eliminated that which was not advantageous to her plan of raising the kids in the admonition of the Lord. The children were growing up very well and Alexis was often complimented for doing such a great job raising them, even though she was fully aware that she was not a perfect parent and she had bad days occasionally, she still tried hard and made a concerted effort to educate herself on how to be a better parent on a continual basis, attending all seminars or free classes regarding child rearing. The kids were smart, well behaved and loved God.

Her mind skipped forward to one Sunday at church services. She was sitting with her friend Calahan, who was one of the men she had briefly dated years ago, but was now only friends with. He had walked to the restroom during the invitation song and from the time he went to the restroom, to the time he returned, a man had gone forward on the other side of the auditorium asking for prayers. He stated his wife had left him because he had decided to become a Christian.

Alexis looked at the stranger's face; she could see his eyes. She glanced around the room curious if anyone else saw what she was seeing. To her, his countenance appeared messed up. The place where his eyes were had the semblance of holes containing darkness that would go on indefinitely if you fell in them. He looked unstable. She recognized this look as being troubled only and could not assign it as anything else; she did not yet know any better and did not understand the depth to which the eyes were a light unto the soul.

As Cal returned, Alexis leaned over to him. "That guy's wife left him because he became a Christian." Cal looked over at him. "Really?" He responded, interested but not surprised. Cal had seen too much in his lifetime to be surprised by much of anything.

A few months later, one day in the church parking lot, a friend approached Alexis and said, "I have this friend who really needs some spiritual guidance and a strong spiritual person to be around." Alexis held up the crossed fingers sign to her to ward her off. "No, no, I don't mean as a dating thing, just a friend thing." Alexis had a reputation as being a strong spiritual godly woman, who did not date, and would do nothing on purpose against God's will and her friend thought she might be good for this person to be around.

"Who is it?"

"Kurt."

That was the guy who had gone forward months earlier because his wife left him; the troubled look guy who was now divorced. He had also gone forward again after the first time stating he was struggling with something but did not specify to the church exactly what "it" was.

In reflection, Alexis shook her head slowly left to right as she dried her body off, wrapped her robe around, tying it by her belly button, and plopped down on the bed, turning the TV to some inconsequential show which allowed the movie in her head to continue as she stared at the screen in front of her. She knew where it was going and said a prayer of thanks to God for delivering her from the most horrible experience of her life.

Nothing became of that particular conversation in the parking lot but months later as Alexis passed Kurt on the front steps of the church building, she heard a conversation about him needing a place to park his lawn mower. The only information she knew about him was he was someone who had been baptized and gave the appearance of wanting to change his life for God. Alexis remembered the way he looked when he went forward, however, she was cognizant of how a person could change their life for God, after all, she had gone from being an atheist to being a strong believer who was well respected in that light. And who was she to judge someone's motives? She remembered the scripture that says, man looks at the outward appearance but God looks at the heart. Besides, the troubled look appeared to be gone and when a person changes their life for God, it is a good thing so she was willing to assist if it meant furthering that goal along for someone else; her intentions were good.

In the hotel room now, she thought about how things might have been different if she had also kept in mind the scripture that says, ye shall know them by their fruits. If she had only given it enough time!

Kurt had sold his house after his divorce and was now in an apartment. She on the other hand, had built a house two years ago after working hard as a single mom to save money and had an empty garage. Seeing this as an opportunity to serve the Lord by helping another church member, she interjected that she had an empty garage and would be glad to provide space for his mower. Besides, she needed her lawn mowed. It would be a reciprocal meeting of needs. Sounded good, almost like the Lord himself had provided the opportunity; thus the beginnings of a relationship.

On occasion, Kurt and Alexis would go to lunch after he mowed her grass but Alexis made sure it was not thought of as a date because she was not interested in dating, and if she was, it certainly would not be with him. One afternoon, when they were sitting at a restaurant eating barbeque, Alexis looked across the table at his face, which for a brief moment turned into a swine face. She looked away. It was confusing to her and surreal but she recognized the image. It made her think of the time a couple years ago when she

21

was struggling with desiring reconciliation with her ex-husband who was not a Christian. When a person has children with someone, regardless of the situation, extinguishing tempting thoughts of reconciliation is difficult because out of love for the kids, there is a desire for them to have both their mommy and daddy around all the time. She also struggled with the guilt of tearing her family apart because of her sin before she was a Christian.

Alexis had dreamed that she and her ex were in a vehicle traveling down a mountainous road similar to the Grand Canyon. They had reconciled and were together; the ex was driving and she was in the passenger's seat. Suddenly the vehicle fell off of a huge cliff that had no barriers and was quickly approaching a sea of light tan colored sand at the bottom. Alexis came out of the vehicle as if she was not housed in a physical body anymore right before the car hit bottom and she was flying up and away while looking down behind her. It was weird though, it was not like she had to physical turn around and look down to see like we would have to do in a physical body; there was no barrier to just seeing, wide open; no head to turn around, no tilt downward to see. She watched the car get swallowed up by quicksand and disappear along with her ex who was also out of the car now. He had turned into a swine and was franticly trying to gain his footing while quickly sinking being buried alive by the sand. She will never forget what the swine looked like as it violently tried to avoid being consumed. The ordeal was over in seconds with no sign of either her ex or the car as she flew upward and away into the sky. After that dream, the thought of

22

reconciliation was not so tempting for her as she interpreted the dream to mean that she was not suppose to reconcile with her ex because they were going in two different spiritual directions and he would lead her directly to hell.

Now she was looking at another swine but she was not dreaming; it was a vision, that was certain. Was this God's way of communicating with her to tell her danger was imminent and not to proceed forward in a relationship with this person? She did not intend to date him or get involved in a romantic way; however, she knew the swine face was a warning. It made an impact on the way she viewed Kurt. She tucked the pig image away in her data bank, not quite sure where to file it because she was not planning to consider a more serious relationship with him other than the acquaintance they had. It confused her to say the least. If she were not turned off to a relationship with him already, the swine face image would have certainly changed that.

The next day at work she mentioned the experience to one of her coworkers she was close to. The woman opined in addition to being a vicious, contemptible, disgusting person, swine also represented spiritual demarcation between good and evil, which confirmed Alexis' speculation about the whole thing. It actual meant a little more than that, however, Alexis would not realize this until years down the road.

Begging for sleep now in her hotel room, Alexis wanted to hit "stop" on her mind's remote control, which steered her movie. It had been a long day for her considering she was up before the sun, drove one hundred miles to get to the speaking engagement, and then practiced her presentation once before the assembly started, but she knew that her movie would only stop if she let it play all the way through or fell asleep and considering the fact that she was not asleep yet, the movie continued. Her tiredness tried to fast forward it along, skipping many details along the way. Eventually she would learn to control this movie, instead of it controlling her but she was not there yet.

CHAPTER TWO

Time would go on, and Kurt would project the image that he was growing spiritually and living for God never letting any nefarious traits show in his personality. He would fix things for Alexis and she started to look forward to their time together. It just so happened that acts-of-service was one of her love languages. Eventually, the swine face image was tucked away so far in the data bank it became covered by deception and deemed ineffectual. The kids were getting older and spending more time with their friends and her ex had come back to town by now which meant the children spent most of their weekends with their dad leaving Alexis alone. For the past seven years, she had not experienced loneliness as a single mother until recently as she longed for adult companionship. Kurt and Alexis' friendship grew and Alexis' error in judgment led her to believe that Kurt was a gift from God. She began missing Kurt when they were not together and eventually they would start officially dating.

As a hedge, she did suggest they have Bible studies together that would allow her to see where he was spiritually which they did a couple times a week. As far as she could outwardly discern he was on the up and up and she felt mistakenly confident that she had scrutinized him well enough that if he were insincere, she would have recognized the hypocrisy. The only problem with this method was that the experts say it takes two years to completely get to know someone and Alexis thought she had done it in months. Consistency over time is what the experts say to look for. Be anxious for nothing…she thought.

During one of their Bible study meetings, they began talking about qualities that people should possess in order to be a blessing in someone else's life. In the "mentally" category, they both devised a list they agreed on. Alexis had contributed that a person should have at least a high school education, and have something they are good at that provides self-esteem. Kurt stated a person should be stable emotionally, not jealous but trusting, not over-reactive but calm, and loyal. These were all clues that Alexis was not educated enough to recognize. He was describing the opposite of what he was; describing the traits in her that he wanted for himself but was incapable of having. In the category of "physically", they both agreed that a person should not be obese and make every effort to be in good physical health. Unbeknownst to Alexis, Kurt had lost thirty pounds during the past year because he fasted from all sweets and prayed to God for Alexis to be his. "Spiritually", Alexis confirmed that a person should have a desire to please God above their self and show their sincerity to God by how they lived and what was important to them. Kurt affirmed that a person should be strong in their faith and be servant minded.

Alexis really believed this relationship was from the Lord, subconsciously dismissing the swine face to be of a time in Kurt's life, which no longer seemed to exist or signify who he was. Here was a man who claimed to be and seemed to be a Christian, and who wanted to take her and her children on as his responsibility knowing she had come from an atheistic ungodly background. Alexis was wide off the mark in seeing their relationship as a blessing instead of what it really was, what he really was.

She was falling in love and who wouldn't fall in love with a guy who appeared to be the ideal man? He was always willing to serve in whatever capacity she needed, never disagreed with her, and complimented her on her cooking and the way her kids behaved, seemed interested in spiritual things and growth, and was thought of by others to be a good guy. There might have been some hesitancy on her part if people had expressed concern about the merger but important people in her life whom she trusted seemed to approve of him and them as a couple, therefore, she proceeded without caution; he was so easy to be around and they had discussed so many issues and he seemed to agree with all of them. For instance, when she shared the fact that she didn't have television and would never have television, he was good with that.

Alexis was ready to give herself to a man in a way she had not yet done as a believer, in a way she had never done in her life, being submissive, focusing on their wants and needs instead of her own. Sacrificing and serving for someone else's happiness, experiencing intimacy of love in the flesh, doing whatever possible to make a relationship successful, looking her best at all times for him, considering that person more important than herself.

The love she felt with God was spiritual, not physically tangible. But here before her was a person who caused her emotions to emulate a little of what she had with God; it could be mirrored in the flesh, someone to hold, to love, to be loved by. She thought this was the true purpose of physical marriage, to imitate our spiritual relationship with God.

However, people have flaws, weaknesses, are not always concerned with what is good for us, sometimes selfish, and can lead us away from God. On the other hand, God would never lead us any where that is not good for us, He wants what is best for us, loves us even when we do not deserve it, and never makes a mistake. So why do we foolishly try to recreate the divine using the sinful nature of man to do so? And what is it that blinds us to ignore this fact so that we fall in love more often than not with the wrong person or with whoever is willing? Our inborn desire, that primordial drive to love and be loved must be what causes us to senselessly take risks in love we would not otherwise take, for without it…

As an atheist, Alexis had been a selfish person, except when it came to her children and outside of that, had never desired to make sacrifices for anyone else's happiness in the way she now desired. Most men would give their right arm to have a wife who was willing to serve like this and Alexis was bound and determined to be that woman especially considering the fact that she was convinced this was a blessing from God. This motivated her all the more to aspire to the Proverbs thirty-one scriptures whereby the woman of the house, among other things, arises before the sun to provide food for her family.

Recently, there had been someone walking around her house in the middle of the night, at one point shinning a flashlight through her kitchen window scanning the living room. This frightened her and the thought of having a man in the house to protect her became even more attractive; she felt safer when Kurt was there. It seemed that everything was pointing to the fact that it was time for her to take the plunge into this relationship.

As a Christian woman Alexis was very strict about how she lived and who she spent time with, never mind the caliber of man she would consider marrying; for a man to win her was quite a feat and Kurt appeared to be that man. No-one had even come close to winning that part for six years, and she had not even dated during that time. Kurt would be winning the heart of a woman who was an exquisite cook, an immaculate housekeeper, a mother who disciplined and controlled her children, a strong confident Christian woman desiring excellence in all she did, with dreams and a positive outlook on life.

Approximately one year after the swine imagery, Kurt and Alexis would become husband and wife and all would look like a fairy tale. They started dating in July, were engaged in October, and married in January. Kurt seemed interested in joining Alexis down the lifestyle path she had paved before him as a Christian and a parent; all appeared well; a smooth transaction. It was like she was driving a train; he approved of all the attached train cars, and wanted to climb aboard to help her get to her destination because he also desired the same destination. In that case, why would she stop someone from riding the train? Eventually, once comfortable though, she was anxious for him to take the wheel, switching body over and under body, the same way she would switch drivers while a vehicle was still traveling down the road, letting her slip into the passenger seat, and fulfill her role as a Christian wife and mother, submissive to the leader of the family in the driver's seat.

The wedding, which was a winter wedding, was announced and everyone was excited for both of them, stating that they were made for each other. Due to work schedules, their honeymoon would take place one month after the wedding allowing them more time. They arrived back home the same way they left, like two love birds in a nest not wanting to leave the other.

One of the things Alexis enjoyed about the winter was sleeping with the windows open slightly so that it became cold in the house but warm under the blankets. Kurt told her this was what he liked also. Therefore, this was what they did and that first winter together as newlyweds was such a wonderful time.

However, the following winter was a different story. Kurt insisted the windows be totally closed up at night and the heat turned on so that the house was always at seventy-six degrees. Alexis recognized it as a contradiction to what he had told her the first winter. She contemplated why she did not detect back then that Kurt was superficially willing to please her and artificially agreed with everything all the time.

Once settled after the honeymoon, their routine was established. After work, they would go for a family bike ride, and then Alexis would prepare dinner. When the kids were done showering, they would read from the Bible or a book the kids picked out, they would have prayer time, then the kids would go to bed and Kurt and Alexis would have their together time. This schedule would be interrupted only on occasion depending on what school or church activity was in session at the time. Never did it occur to Alexis as boring or tedious; raising her children was rewarding, especially when they showed signs of maturity. She was committed and in it for the long haul knowing that the benefits would come only by the investment of time.

Shortly after they were married, a note appeared on Alexis' pillow: "Good morning my love. I will think about you all day, I hate being away from you and I anticipate the time I can see you later. You have made me so happy and made me feel so wanted. God is awesome and has answered my prayers in giving me the right bait to catch you. Love your blessed husband."

Alexis felt complete as a woman, so fulfilled. Kurt's presence in her life caused greater happiness than she had expected. Before him, she felt whole as a Christian but had not experienced the joy a woman finds in becoming one with a man in the most perfect manifestation of the husband wife relationship. For the first time in her life the quintessential realization of Christian matrimony was self evident in the overflow of perpetual exultation her heart radiated on a daily basis. Everyone around her noticed it, and made mention of such. Calahan, someone who did not give out compliments very often commented, "Marriage looks good on you."

It was not the reason she had married, she had married because she fell in love, but no longer would she have to be alone to tackle life's difficulties anymore. Whether it was positive or negative, she now had someone to share things with; life's little twist and turns seemed easier with someone at your side and becoming one with some body else was never so appealing. She was glowing and felt like she had reached the pinnacle of joy in her life. The only thing that compared was the birth of her children and her relationship with God.

For the most part, Alexis conducted her life the same way after the wedding as she had done before the wedding, making exception to her responsibilities as a wife with more cooking, cleaning, laundry and the physical union with her husband. It was exhausting considering her full time job, but she delighted in it because after all, this relationship was a blessing from God. Still eager for Kurt to take the wheel of the train, she began to relinquish the steering mechanisms slowly, relying on him, trusting him to lead the family, however, she never reached the full potential of allowing this transition to be completed. The reasons why she didn't feel comfortable doing this confused her. She should have known him better before she married him. She knew there was much at stake and she was not willing to commit herself to a course from which there was no return if he was not going to lead them to a godly place; her kids' lives were at stake.

In electricity, a bridge is used to measure resistances and frequencies by comparing the effect of the unknown element with that of known or standard elements in the circuit. This was in essence what Alexis was doing with Kurt before she was willing to totally surrender control, and what she thought she had done efficiently while they were dating but she hadn't given it enough time to work properly. Obviously, the results of her original measurement were skewed and the forthcoming results eroded the confidence gained in the beginning. She would eventually learn why the experts say to date someone for at least two years before you marry them.

It was roughly five months after the wedding when the older man who had taken Alexis' daughter on a trip to the springs would be convicted of having sexual intercourse with his granddaughter and sentenced to fifteen years in prison.

Alexis freaked out at the news and was on heightened awareness as she saw Kurt sitting on the couch with her daughter, who was pre-puberty, about eight years old. Her daughter was on Kurt's lap because he had encouraged her to sit there, and Kurt had a blanket over them. She had seen the red flags with the old man and she was right. Every bone in her body had been correct; every feeling she had was accurate; now she felt it again.

"Oh no you don't." Alexis said to Kurt.
"What?" He asked seemingly without a clue.
"The blanket. I don't want you sitting there with her on your lap with a blanket over the two of you."

Kurt became angry and although Alexis did not want to upset Kurt she felt what she was seeing was a red flag and preserving her daughter's innocence was more important than not making him mad.

Approximately two days later, as Alexis was preparing dinner, she wondered what Kurt was doing in her daughter's bedroom. She could hear them, the door was open and everything sounded ok, but she was still operating with enhanced senses from the news about the conviction she knew could have left her daughter a victim. Alexis walked from the kitchen around the corner toward her daughter's bedroom and saw Kurt lying on the floor on his stomach with his forearms propping up his rib cage area off of the floor. He was looking at her daughter who was sitting there to the right of him with her legs spread apart playing with something similar to the way a child would sit on the floor and play jacks between their legs. Why wasn't he paying attention to her son? To Alexis, it appeared as if Kurt was staring into her daughter's private area even though she had long shorts on and you could not see up them so it did not make sense; was he undressing her with his eyes? Still, the attention he was giving her daughter as opposed to her son set off an alarm in her head that invoked her protective mode.

"What are you doing?" She asked Kurt.

"What do you mean?" He could tell by the look on her face and the sound of her voice she was insinuating he was doing something wrong. He quickly got up off the floor and walked into the other room.

Alexis followed him. "It looks like you are staring between her legs." It sounded ridiculous to her after she said it.

"What?" He screamed. "You think I am staring at your daughter's crotch?"

"That's what it looked like."

34

Kurt went into a rage attack, yelling that she had a serious problem, and Alexis made it worse by trying to explain herself and talk to him when he did not want to talk. He picked up his keys and wallet and left the house incensed. Why was he reacting this way she wondered? Why was he not talking to her, reasoning with her?

Alexis was confused. Was she imagining things because of what had transpired with the old man? Or did she really have a sensitive discerning ability that God had blessed her with to tell when things were not quite right? If that was the case, then why did she get involved with Kurt in the first place? What was going on? She knew that guilty people typically over react when caught in something and it bothered her tremendously that Kurt had done just that. Why did he get up off of the floor so fast like he was caught doing wrong if he was not? This was her first serious criticism of him, their first real fight and Kurt's first display of uncontrolled rage which reminded her of Ivan. Even the language he used during the rage attack reminded her of Ivan.

After several hours, Kurt called from his mother's house. He apologized for getting so mad, stated he did not do anything wrong, at which time Alexis apologized for accusing him of what she thought she saw. The whole experience was chalked up to the conviction of the old man and Alexis' intensified emotional state, but there was still a question in her mind. Deep down, part of her did not believe him and never would. For now though, she had to move ahead. What else was there to do? Was she going to divorce a man after five months of marriage because she thought she saw some sketchy hint of perversion that she could not prove knowing she was on red alert from the conviction of the old man? How ridiculous!

A few weeks later, there would be one more incident in relation to her daughter, making three all together, that cemented her thoughts of mistrust toward Kurt. She did not want to believe it and tried for a long time to justify it, or make excuses about what she saw and heard. Kurt and Alexis were sitting by the front door of the house and her daughter was running and playing in the street in front of them with a friend. Both girls were approximately eight years old and they looked so innocent, playing and laughing. Kurt was looking toward the girls and said, "Mmm, mmm, mmm." Much the same way you would look at a piece of chocolate cake with desire and in a way that made her think he forgot she was there like he was delusional and in a trance of sorts.

"What did you say?" Alexis asked in disbelief.

Kurt seemed startled. "I didn't say anything." He had that angry sound in his voice once again, that Alexis was all too familiar with by now.

"Yes you did. You went Mmm, mmm, mmm."

"No I didn't. You are crazy; you've got problems and need to be committed." Kurt stood up and walked off toward the garage angrily. The rest of the day was filled with tension between them with Alexis in an utter state of stupefaction. She could understand if maybe Kurt would have said something like, "You know, they are growing up so fast"; or "We're gonna need a gun to run the boys

36

off". But his obvious over-reaction to the whole thing was a huge red flag for Alexis. Was he so perverted that he slipped in and out of being delusional?

Alexis and Kurt had planned on having a child of their own but as Alexis prayed that particular evening, she asked God to never allow her to get pregnant if in fact she was right about what she thought, vowing to not let her daughter ever be alone with Kurt. This was not a casual relationship from which she could disconnect as she had done with the old man; she was married to this guy now. The uncertainty ran through her mind cutting pathways to the different possible outcomes.

Even though it appeared their relationship recovered from these incidents it never really did and it seemed to Alexis that from this point forward, things would never be the same in their marriage; it was a turning point. Kurt developed a growing hatred for Alexis that would come out through verbal abuse, rage attacks, put downs and absolute contempt and difficulty. Alexis' trust of him vanished with every passing hour and caused her to be more critical of him. They could not get through two weeks without fighting about something stupid and he was difficult to deal with at best. She figured he hated her because she noticed something he did not want her to notice: that he was perverted. Months later he had made a comment that he would not do anything to her daughter because she would kill him. Alexis found this odd, seeing as how his first reason for not wanting to do something like that should be the fact that he had no desire for little girls.

What was really happening with Kurt was the real person was coming out because he could not continue to suppress it, however, Alexis unaware of the purposeful deceit from the beginning, blamed herself for their trouble because of her accusations of his intent. At the same time though, she knew what she saw and heard in spite of how he denied it. Even so, she tried to understand that if someone accused her of something she was not guilty of, she would undoubtedly be upset, and it would probably ruin the friendship, in particular if it were of a sexual nature. It would affect her greatly, and even cause bitterness to set in. She had not really accused him of anything, and felt she was just being protective of her daughter and could not know his heart or prove his intent. Nevertheless, her intuition had always served her well and to her knowledge, had never been erroneous. Now doubting her instinct, she apologized to Kurt, because there was nothing else to do, and tried to move on. But why would God allow her to marry a man like this, if in fact it was true? Had she successfully been led astray? Maybe she was over-reacting; imagining things. She prayed about it constantly. Perhaps if Kurt did have ulterior motives or inappropriate thoughts about her daughter, she could change the way he thought about it, convicting his thinking patterns. If anyone was strong enough to help someone mature, she was. Perhaps this was what God wanted her to do, a ministry of sorts. Although she would confess to a close friend that because the old man was not successful at getting to her daughter, Satan was now trying to get to her through her husband, someone on the inside who had infiltrated his way into her home. Her friend claimed she was being melodramatic and paranoid. This assertion helped to calm her down a bit.

There were times Kurt and Alexis would get along well and were happy. Inevitably, though, something would happen to ruin it. As seepage from a broken sewer line, personality traits began to surface from Kurt that had previously been purposely concealed. Alexis thought her criticism of him was the event that caused the break in the line and began noticing that Kurt would disrupt every attempt she made at having order in her home, especially with the children. For instance, during prayer time at dinner, he would play like a two year old child, not taking prayer seriously, trying to get the kids to laugh and play with him, squeezing hands, kicking under the table, etc., then when the kids would get in trouble for it he would point at them and say, "Ha, Ha! You got in trouble." Alexis did not know how to respond and was agitated at the immature and sadistic behavior.

He was nullifying her accomplishments in teaching the kids to have reverence toward God and appropriate behavior. When she would correct the kids, he would accuse her out loud in front of them of taking the fun out of everything, trying to get them to feel the way he was acting toward her. She felt as if he was trying to turn the kids against her. Then when she would defend herself he would start to humiliate and criticize her with abusive words.

This irritated her for obvious reasons, but primarily because Kurt was trying to turn it all around to make it seem like she had a problem when in fact she knew there were people who were even more structured, strict and serious than she was. Besides, reverence for God was something a Christian should possess; talking to God in prayer was not an appropriate place to play. She constantly wondered if the difficulty had to do with her recognition of what she perceived to be intended evil toward her daughter.

In her mind, she never believed the words he hurled at her, like "stupid", "no fun", and various profanities, because there were too many confirmations from other people and blessings showing she had done a good job at raising her kids and living life. When he projected profanity at her, she would rebuke him as a Christian, then he would say, "What are you gonna do about it now? You're already married to me, you baby?" It was the ultimate slap in the face! How could she hold someone accountable if they dismissed the very thing they are accountable to? It was exasperating because Kurt seemed incapable of talking through any conflict and never understood any other point of view but his own. Another symptom that Alexis was not educated enough to recognize. His behavior was so childish. The last time she observed name-calling was in her kids' grade school. Instead of feeling like she was in an adult-to-adult relationship, she felt like she was in another adult-to-child relationship, except her children were more mature than he was.

Alexis knew there had to be order otherwise you had complete chaos. Kurt seemed to thrive on chaos becoming hateful toward order of any kind. He would then accuse Alexis of sucking life and enjoyment out of situations when she tried to institute order. Alexis knew this too was not true because she had joy and life in abundance before Kurt arrived on the scene. She began to recognize that Kurt often accused her of what he was guilty of. Alexis was not educated enough to know that this trait is indicative of a severe personality disorder. Kurt had not demonstrated any hint of this behavior before their real first fight at five months into the marriage.

Why was Kurt so obstreperous? Alexis did not understand but was observant enough to realize that it had started after the first time she had seriously criticized him and she knew it had something to do with that. The functional range of her perception of the dynamics occurring in their relationship would not reach any beneficial level until approximately two years into their Sisyphean marriage.

The times of fighting would be contradicted by times of excessive compliments and affection that would occur after Kurt was done vomiting his rage onto Alexis. It was similar to the way a kitten would play with a catnip mouse. The kitten loved the catnip and at the same time had to swat it around, chase it, catch the mouse, extend its claws into it, bite it and then leave it, discarding it for use at a later time, thereby contradicting its claim of loving catnip in the first place. It has been said that love is an action and that unless verbal claims of love are transferred into action backing up the claim, the verbal claim is nullified and not based in reality, but rather based in unreality and insane.

41

When she would discuss some of the happenings of the marriage with friends, not really knowing how to explain it, she would be told that she was being too sensitive, or doing something to invoke the behavior, and that the security of the marriage would grow with time. Eventually, she would stop talking to anyone about it at all except God.

She was not aware that using her to rage would be an ongoing need of Kurt's. Nor was she aware that he subconsciously considered it her responsibility to meet this need because she was the one closest to him. In addition, she was not privy to the programming transpiring within her own mind: excessive verbal abuse versus excessive praise. Eventually through research she would discover that the psychological techniques he subconsciously used to try to break her down emotionally were equivalent to the same methods used for consciously torturing a victim to conform their thinking patterns, causing them to regress psychologically. It was a contest between him, the tormentor and her, the victim. He would humiliate her, verbally abuse her, betray her, leave her feeling helpless, constantly expose her to ambiguous situations or contradictory messages and bully her. This in effect, was a complete description of how her husband treated her, especially the ambiguous situations, and is exactly how torture methods work.

Most people think of torture in terms of physical abuse that is inflicted on a victim, but torture can also be emotional or mental. In addition, if the tormentor can get the victim to feel like they are inflicting pain upon themselves, they will most likely injure the victim's will to resist, whereas if the victim feels like the injury is being inflicted from outside himself, his strength to resist will increase. Kurt was achieving success in getting Alexis to look inward at her self as the cause of their marriage difficulty. He would purposely allow a period of getting along so that he could confuse Alexis by surprising her with his outbursts which worked to his advantage for his coercive methods.

Unknowingly, Alexis was vulnerable to Kurt's programming because she was so willing to please her husband, and had seen her mother mentally, emotionally, verbally and mildly physically abused for years when she was a young child and teenager. She had no idea she was in bondage as that little girl, unable to help her mother. She recognized abusive behavior right away but subconsciously was powerless to do anything about it, except argue. Defending herself when injured was the mode her machine was stuck in. This provided the perfect outlet for Kurt to respond with rage. Defending herself was exactly what he needed her to do which automatically provided the excuse to unload onto her and she was caught up in the cycle not even realizing she was enabling him to continue his patterns of abuse. Instinctively she was providing the conduit for his anger because of her acquired mode of response toward his behavior.

As she grew in her understanding of how he worked, she learned that giving him a taste of his own medicine, treating him the way he treated her in other words, resulted in a higher level of communication with him not otherwise attained. Not that he was easier to deal with, but he seemed to get something out of it that prompted a quicker end to the fighting. This method was totally against what she had been taught as a Christian, but worked with Kurt. It was so weird to her because it was as if he was begging her inside his soul to treat him this way, like he needed to be verbally abused back to survive; little did Alexis know he really did need it to survive. Nor did she know that the way he acted was contagious.

So when they were arguing one time, Alexis said she did not want to talk anymore, which was what he typically said to her. She prepared to take her daily shower and looked forward to it because a hot shower on a cold winter day was something that pleasured her. After getting all soaped up, she noticed the water stopped. After a minute of wondering what happened, she began to get cold and feel uncomfortable because she had just soaped up her face and could not open her eyes; she had not rinsed the soap off yet. She stood there, eyes closed, yelling for Kurt.

"You're gonna talk to me now." Kurt said to her as he walked in the bathroom from the garage where he had turned off all the water to the entire house. "I'll turn the water back on after you talk to me." He was laughing at her standing in the tub all soapy and shivering, not even offering her a towel.

Alexis could not believe he would do such a thing or the supercilious look on his face once she grabbed the towel and wiped her eyes which stung from the soap. "Kurt this is abusive, why are you doing this? You tell me all the time that you do not want to talk anymore and just expect me to wait." She was not sure if she should cry or get mad, but was slowly realizing that there were serious issues in her marriage and with him.

During the times of verbal affliction, Kurt appeared to become a different person. His face and eyes took on another appearance and there was always profanity spewing forth from him like he was demon possessed. Alexis began to suspect split personality syndrome or severe anger issues but was still not quite sure what was going on. All she knew was that she was miserable when they fought but felt so good when they made up. She was strong enough not to be totally crippled by the abuse; however, she was still in bondage to it because the emotional and mental patterns along with the enabling were in place and efficiently working. Alexis was glad that most of the fighting occurred when the children were with their father but they too had been the target of Kurt's rage from time to time and had witnessed the arguing on occasion.

In the hotel room, as her head nodded off to the right and back up again, Alexis thought about how hard she had tried to please Kurt in listening to his conglomerate of critical accusations. In wanting to please him, she would try to loosen up. Maybe she was too strict with the children; no one is beyond needing improvement. All the same, she would ask herself repeatedly, if that was true, why was God blessing her life and the lives of her children beyond what she could even imagine. Why did people compliment her, regarding the children who were wonderful kids and pleasant to be around. Why was she and her children respected if what he said was true?

Blindly she tried to communicate and conflict resolve their differences in rational, logical ways. He thought everyone was like him, operating in chaos with a little structure thrown in for good measure and would accuse Alexis of not being normal. Alexis on the other hand, knew that most people were more like her, if not more so. These were the types of truths she clung to which helped her survive. This is what her marriage felt like at this point, a lesson in survival.

Most of the people she knew were responsible, had steady jobs, and conducted their lives in serious ways, with a little chaos thrown in on occasion, like a vacation for instance. Her attempts to discuss this or any other matter with Kurt, coming to some logical conclusion, as critical thinking teaches, never worked and were always defeated by arguments, yelling, and chasing rabbits that were not even in the neighborhood when the conversation first began. Kurt's expert ability to ping pong an issue in conversation was superior to that of anyone she had ever known and worked to obfuscate her on a continual basis. It was a game she could not win no matter how well she played; she did not realize this yet. The way Kurt's words flowed forth with ease was so convoluted she could not keep up. Within the first two years of their marriage, Kurt had left several times during these wars of words and being sucked into the emotional vortex, she had kicked him out once.

The movie had now gone as far in her mind as it would for tonight as Alexis' head finally fell off to the side not to return to its upright position until the rising of the sun.

Lessons From The Lawn - Part I

The most popular grass in the southern state of Florida is St. Augustine grass. It is beautiful when nurtured properly. This grass is a vine that shoots off runners from itself, spreading out, growing in length, and putting down new roots. It's thick and strong. From Alexis' point of view, if someone had never walked bare foot on a well manicured St. Augustine lawn they were missing out on something wonderful. The sensation was one that Alexis looked forward to when her house was being built. After she moved in, it was one of the first things she did: walk barefoot on the lawn soaking in the joy of what her feet were feeling. Someone else might think it trivial or foolish, however, there are different things in life that bring us joy in various ways depending on personal preference and this was one of the minor pleasures that Alexis felt was a blessing in her life. She had never had anything so nice growing up, no new house, no beautiful lawn. Now she was an adult and had saved enough money to build her own house through hard work. Yes, taking care of the lawn was important to her. Was it a sin to want to take care of that which God had blessed her with? Was it a sin to enjoy the sensation of cushy dark green cold grass under her bare feet?

When Alexis first moved into the house she knew that she would not have the knowledge to take care of her own lawn, therefore, she hired a company to come by every month and provide whatever the lawn seemed to need. It worked well; she paid a fee, they took care of the lawn, Alexis walked barefoot on the grass.

On the west side of the house there was a thirty foot easement leading to a drainage ditch, which when full of water was referred to as the "crick" by Alexis and her children; a child's wonderland full of tadpoles, minnows, sometimes snakes, and deer tracks nearby. Alexis would never have to worry about anyone building on that side of her but on the east side of the house, there was a lot for sale. With only ten feet of land on the edge belonging to Alexis she knew when the lot next to her was developed it would be close quarters. For their first three years in the house it was not a worry and this property remained as woods but then the lot was purchased, a house was built, and a lawn was planted. Incidentally, this coincided with the time Alexis and Kurt began hanging out together.

The two lawns met at that ten-foot property mark with no barrier between them and Alexis did not have the knowledge which would allow her to consider the ramifications of this union; for one was St. Augustine and one was Bahia, a much lower grade grass than St. Augustine and very different. For half a year after the new neighbors moved in, both lawns gave the appearance of being healthy; no one suspected that microscopic observation was needed.

Alexis had not educated herself about St. Augustine lawn care, thereby setting herself up to fail due to the absence of knowledge, which is true ignorance. Instead, she relied on the wisdom of others to achieve the outcome she desired. Sometimes

48

this works and sometimes it doesn't. When the anticipated outcome did not meet her standards, she confronted the responsible entity. When her neighbor stopped by one day to tell her that the lawn company she had hired, came by, and put a bill on her door without performing any service, she did not think twice about firing them. Alexis did not doubt the truthfulness of her neighbor's accusation because the lawn had begun to show subtle signs of neglect; brown spots for instance that substantiated her neighbor's claim. She did not hesitate at transferring lawn care responsibility to Kurt her new husband who had claimed to be self-employed at one time in his life as a lawn maintenance technician.

CHAPTER THREE

Kurt did not have children but had stated that he wanted them and Alexis thought it would be good for him to experience the parenting role; maybe it would help him to grow up and mature emotionally. She also loved him and desired to create a life together with him although she never forgot her prayer.

After six months of trying, Alexis asked her doctor who obliged, for a mild fertility drug to aid the so far unsuccessful process along. It was now prime time in the procedure of conception, for his sperm to meet with her egg to form a baby.

Alexis was sitting on the toilet, urinating after having sex with her husband. She noticed there was no ejaculation present or usual smell as she wiped. She flushed the toilet and walked back into the bedroom.

"Did you ejaculate?" She asked him embarrassed at the thought that he might have faked it. She heard of women doing that from time to time but wondered whether men did it too. Alexis had been suspicious of this in the past.

"Yes."

"Well, there was nothing there, I mean, usually it's messy, you know, I can tell."

"I don't know what to say, I'm sure I did, I mean I thought I did. Maybe there was not much of it."

"How can you not know if you did or didn't?"

"I don't know, I thought I did." He equivocated in an irritated voice.

This would not be the last time Kurt would lie about ejaculation; it happened again but Alexis was unsure how to handle it and talking about it just aggravated him and it was not the sort of thing to talk to a friend about so she never told anyone. She thought maybe he was just too embarrassed to tell her that the new had worn off already and he could not keep up with the demand that trying to conceive a child required so she excused it and tucked it away like a neat little hanky in a pocket to be used at a later time.

This whole bizarre situation coincided with sexual fantasy talking. "Tell me about the times in high school with your boyfriend." Kurt asked as he and Alexis lay in bed together, caressing each other. Like most young people from her generation, she was sexually promiscuous in her youth long before she became a Christian, even though it was mild compared to some of her friends, and Kurt liked to hear about it.

Alexis thought this was an odd request for a Christian man, but was willing to please her husband allowing what she suspected to be right to override what her husband desired at the time. He became so affectionate and his physical desire for her intensified so much when she talked about having sex with other men that she could not resist; it made her feel that he wanted her. Why she so desperate to feel that he wanted her that she would turn to evil? Or was she just so confused because of his manipulations that she was not sure of her own identity anymore? A scripture played across her mind like a ticker tape alerting her to never look back at life before God and glamorize it or think it was good, but the desire to please her husband prevailed over this scripture.

Her mind displayed another scripture competing with the last one that said the woman was created for the pleasure of man. If that were so, and her husband derived sexual pleasure from hearing her talk dirty, then what was she suppose to do? If she obeyed her husband would he then be held responsible for her disobedience to God? Was it, in fact, disobedience to God to talk about having sex with other men if you are married? At one point she told him she did not like talking like a slut and his venomous response to her was that he would not be married to a prude and sex would be boring if they did not do it his way.

It really turned Kurt on when she talked about her past sexual activity and Alexis thought that a wife should please her husband thinking that if they do not get it at home, they will get it somewhere. In addition, the subconscious compartment in the back of her mind told her that if she did everything Kurt wanted sexually, he would leave her daughter alone.

Still she wondered, was talking about ungodly sexual things ok if your husband wanted you to do it? If a Christian woman goes against God by being submissive to her husband, is she subject to God's judgment or is the husband accountable for what he asked the wife to do? So many thoughts wandered through her mind fruitlessly looking for dwelling places, contributing to the confusion there.

For six years Alexis had taught kindergarten age Bible class on Wednesday nights at her church and just because she was now married she had no intentions of giving it up. However, she began to feel that Kurt was getting attached to a woman in his class because of the way he talked about her; it seemed he was almost obsessed with her. This, married to his inability to ejaculate without some kind of perverted or pornographic stimulation, caused Alexis to distrust Kurt. It also made her feel inadequate as a wife, but she knew she was attractive enough; mostly she was confused. So she decided to give up teaching for a while in order to attend classes with him curious about her suspicions and wanting answers to the questions that confused her about Kurt. A woman can tell when their husband is attracted to another woman beyond the acknowledgement of good looks. The trust Alexis had toward Kurt had been injured early and never quite fully repaired, so as suspicious women are, Alexis was on guard and rightly so as she would later discover. After all, she had been on guard with the old man and had been right.

Her name was Priscilla, her husband's name was Pete. Pete often sat downstairs with their young kids in the nursery, which left Priscilla free to sit upstairs in class with Kurt. She was a beautiful woman, opposite Alexis in many ways. Priscilla looked like something out of Playboy magazine from head to toe, but with clothes on. Her blonde hair was long and full of body but not curly; it did not frizz in the rain. Her body measurements would have made any man fall at her feet. She had brilliant blue eyes, perfect skin without make-up, no pimples, perfect cute little feet that were manicured making her sandals all the more attractive. Alexis had never thought about it before but as she observed Priscilla now under a microscope she had to admit that if you were a guy, you would think Priscilla was extremely attractive.

Alexis was more athletic and not voluptuous at all. She felt at ease in jeans and t-shirt and derived pleasure from running a challenging 5-K sweating and spitting like a coal miner. She barely filled out an A cup, her face still broke out before her period, and if she ever wore sandals she felt as if she would get a ticket for disturbing the peace. She could not remember the last time her nails were polished while Priscilla's nails were always well manicured and painted. Priscilla came from a wealthy upbringing and she carried herself likewise; Alexis was raised in poverty. Although they did not see much of each other, except for church functions, the two of them had gotten along fairly well until now.

One particular Wednesday, Kurt and Alexis had been arguing at home prior to Bible class but they went anyway. They took their seats at the table. Alexis had never really noticed all of the differences between her and the other woman as she sat on the opposite side of Kurt from Priscilla. As a matter of fact, Alexis had not really compared herself to any woman in a long time but in this first year of marriage she found herself doing just that; often, to the point of being considered abnormal she thought. It was because of the way Kurt made her feel. Maybe it was the way he continually exaggerated her beauty to the point where she knew he was lying. Or the way he was unable to keep himself from staring at a pretty woman no matter where they were. She saw herself realistically, not in fantasy. She felt she was attractive enough to turn heads when she cleaned up but knew she was not a supermodel as he continually purported. On a scale from one to ten she would give herself a six, which was slightly above average. She knew her legs were in good shape for her age; she was a runner, but on the other hand she knew she had the ugliest knees on the face of the planet due to Osgood Slater's disease. She had accepted it a long time ago; it was ok, and she was fully aware of and comfortable with her strengths and weaknesses realizing that everyone had them. She did not think that people should waste so much time on the things they had no control over, but should instead focus on things they did have control over, like who they were as a person, their aspirations, how they raised their children, how they contributed to society in a positive way, and so on.

So when Kurt would point to a supermodel on a magazine cover and tell her she was better looking than that, at first she would giggle and be flattered, but then it became embarrassing and it would make him mad when she would talk truthfully about herself in conversation like the fact that the skin under her eyes was getting older, thinner and the wrinkles were coming. She wanted to embrace the reality of getting older and wanted him to do it with her accepting the whole thing, not live in some fantasy world.

Sometimes it seemed as if his existence depended on denying reality, like a drug he could not live without. This began to make her feel alienated from him and untrusting of his opinions and words. She could understand a man saying, "Honey, it is ok if you get older I will still love you," or some other reassuring phrase, however, it was inconceivable to her that a husband would actually become angry to the point of rage just because his wife, while taking out her contacts, made a comment about the skin under her eyes beginning to wrinkle. Alexis was stubborn in getting Kurt to see her point about his denial of reality which made getting along with him more difficult. She did not yet know any better.

So here they were in Bible class after a blow up, which was caused by Alexis stating that the skin under her eyes was getting wrinkly, and that blow up had not been resolved yet. Alexis was on one side of Kurt, Priscilla on the other. Kurt was not speaking to Alexis (this was customary behavior for him after a fight he initiated) and barely acknowledged she was there, withholding all forms of affection toward her, including looking at her, like he was punishing her. In contrast to that, he was directing all kinds of attention toward Priscilla including rolling up his gum wrapper and playfully throwing it at her. Alexis arose in anger at this obvious insensitivity and successful attempt to manipulate and walked out of the auditorium to the foyer where she would sit for the remainder of class with no response from Kurt. It was emotional manipulations like this that baffled Alexis for a long time; the truth being concealed for another two years.

After class, they had to stop at Pete and Priscilla's so Pete could give something to Kurt. Pete was in the house and Alexis, Kurt

56

and Priscilla were standing and waiting outside. Priscilla had walked over toward the house for a minute to pick something up off of the ground so her back was turned toward Alexis and Kurt. Alexis was standing to the side of Kurt but a few more inches forward than him. Kurt was watching Priscilla walk, "Nice butt!" He said loud enough for Alexis to hear; she wondered if Priscilla had heard the comment too. Alexis calmly responded, "Who's? Her's or mine?" This, in itself, made Kurt angry. Would it have made any difference what Alexis said? Or was he going to get angry at whatever she said because he needed a release of rage? Alexis was not quite sure anymore but she was stubborn in getting Kurt to see the facts because it was the only logical way she knew to communicate, so she said, "Well, I was not the one you were looking at when you made the comment." Kurt lied and said he was talking about Alexis and then, like a child, called her a name.

Priscilla rejoined them and began to talk about the fact that she use to live across the street. Trying to make the best of a difficult situation, Alexis tried to make small talk and asked how much they charged for rent. She said she never paid rent. Alexis was confused, Priscilla responded, "Let's just say I was really bad back then." Kurt looked at Alexis, she analyzed his body language and face, which seemed to say, "Priscilla is better than you because she use to pay for her rent with sex; you've never done that and that turns me on". Why would he want to display this kind of body language? Was he aware of the message he was relaying right in front of his wife?

Alexis was certain that Kurt was smitten with this woman way beyond a casual infatuation but she did not know the woman enough to determine Priscilla's intentions. Was she even aware of Kurt's interest in her; or the fact that Kurt practically drooled every time he saw her? How could she not be aware? Surely Priscilla was smart enough to notice Kurt's body language and the way he acted around her as opposed to the way he treated Alexis. It does not take a rocket scientist to pick up on this stuff. Later that night Kurt made a point to tell Alexis that her hair tie was frayed but Priscilla's wasn't.

A couple weeks later Kurt invited Pete and Priscilla over for dinner. This in itself almost caused a fight between them. Alexis did not want them to come for dinner because she knew what would happen; however, she had underestimated the whole thing. Kurt was like a schoolboy with his first date bending over backwards to impress Priscilla; playing with her kids like he was up for some father of the year award, when in fact he had made comments in the past that her kids were brats. Constant contradictory messages were the only consistency about him.

They were sitting at the table, dinner was served and everyone had their plates in front of them except Alexis. She handed her plate to Kurt so that he could place it at her seat for her as she was going to return something to the kitchen. Right at the time that Kurt had Alexis' plate in hand, Priscilla asked if they had any margarine instead of real butter. Hearing this and being very eager to please Priscilla, Kurt quickly flung Alexis' plate over to her place

58

and set it down, causing the juice on the plate to splash off onto the upholstered chair, the table and the floor, as he got up and said, "I'll get it." Alexis just looked at him in disbelief. He was totally unaware he had spilled the food and acted as if he had nothing to do with it.

Later when they were leaving, Kurt was following Priscilla asking, "Is there anything else I can do for you? Do you need me to carry something?" He was falling all over himself trying to help her. Alexis wondered if anyone else found this behavior a little odd? Was Pete even cognizant enough to recognize when another man was trying to impress or hit on his wife? Was she loosing her mind? Alexis thought about the history of the three of them. She knew that often times Kurt would hang out with Priscilla when Pete was working. It was a crazy thought but Kurt acted like he was head over heels in love with Priscilla and had always been.

Alexis did not yet know any better so when Pete and Priscilla were gone, she told Kurt he made a fool of himself. "What was that anyway? Slinging my plate across the table so fast, spilling everything?" Of course Kurt was in total denial he had done anything and accused Alexis of having a serious jealousy problem. "You're the one with the problem. Most guys don't get turned on thinking of their wives with another man." It was done. Kurt's rage was set free with these words like a prisoner's bars rolled aside releasing their captive. He grabbed his keys and left the house. Alexis noticed that whenever she would speak the truth he reacted like someone was pouring acid on him and he could not get away fast enough.

Eventually Alexis had an opportunity to ask Priscilla if she could talk with her in private. This came about after she observed Priscilla winking at Kurt. Alexis believed that if she had a problem with someone, that it is best to go directly to that person to talk about it. They had a good talk, about an hour's worth. "I wink at everyone and if Pete was not around, I would not be interested in Kurt, if that's what you are asking." Priscilla even volunteered some information about a couple times when she herself had become jealous when Pete was speaking with an attractive friend who was a single woman, for over an hour at her place of employment.

Later that night when Alexis told Kurt what Priscilla had said about him, his angry response was, "Thanks. Thanks a lot for that." It was as if Alexis had busted his bubble and he became depressed after this. She thought that if he could just face reality he would be set free. "Ye shall know the truth, and the truth will set you free." But it would be two more years before Alexis concluded Kurt would never be able to face reality and that he would perpetually be in bondage to fantasy for the rest of his life.

Although Kurt did not like it, Alexis felt better about the situation after speaking with Priscilla. She felt Priscilla was aware that Kurt was attracted to her and used it for her own ego boost, however, Alexis was confident that Priscilla was not interested in Kurt.

For a moment it would seem like Alexis could ease up and relax, but there was always some incident involving another woman that transpired. The next time was at the baseball fields when Kurt practically threw himself at a girl at least fifteen years younger than himself. Alexis observed not knowing what to do but was coming to the conclusion that Kurt always had to have some other woman he was extracting attention from. She would always ask herself first if it was just her imagination, but it wasn't, and Kurt's problem with women went way beyond the normal noticing of attractive women that most guys experience.[3]

There were also times when Kurt would exhibit inappropriate behavior like the time when they were at a get together at someone's house. Their pretty sixteen-year-old daughter came bopping down the stairs to which Kurt called out loud enough for everyone in the room to hear "Now there's a pretty girl." Everyone stopped talking and looked to see what he was referring to because he had said it so loudly. Alexis knew that it was not one of those comments made by people in respect about how good looking someone's kid was, but a comment made as a man sexually aroused by what he saw. He had tried to cover it up by thinking that if he openly made the comment loudly for everyone to hear, he would not be suspected of hiding anything. Surely a man who had inappropriate thoughts about a sixteen-year-old would not bring attention to that fact by making a public statement that he thought she was pretty. As Alexis turned around and looked at him he tried to carry it off like he was speaking about Alexis, by raising his arm toward the girl at the bottom of the stairs and saying, "And there's a pretty girl also." However, Alexis was standing behind a pillar by the front door when he made the first declaration and knew what he was doing; it was not until Alexis moved that he saw her. There had been other incidents regarding this same girl in the past that had gone into Alexis' data bank and it all seemed very weird to her.

By this time Kurt started talking in his sleep excessively about sexual things and other women. He had just switched jobs and worked around ungodly men who often viewed pornographic magazines at work and ogled at the attractive women who came in. Most of their patrons were women and the comment was made to Alexis in jest one time that "Kurt flirted with all of them".

"You're so pretty. Don't tell Alexis." Kurt said in clear words as Alexis woke up in the dark wondering if he was talking to her. She quickly realized he was talking in his sleep and became irritated at the fact that he was obviously speaking with some woman in his dream and did not want her to know. Dreams always made her curious about what was going on inside the brain at the time.

Still clueless about Kurt's schemes and how he worked, feelings of protectiveness were invoked in her and she thought that if any woman was going to turn her husband on it was her. God tells us He is a jealous God. In other words, He does not want anyone else to come before Him. Alexis was a jealous wife in that she did not want anyone to take top billing above her. Therefore, not realizing the manipulation occurring, the craving to be everything to her husband intensified. This way, someone else did not have to be, and he would not have an excuse to put anyone else in that position. When she mentioned the dream to him the next day, he defended himself by saying he did not have control over his mind when he was sleeping. Alexis thought to herself, "You don't even have control over yourself when you are awake!"

As a single Christian, Alexis had given every area of her being to God, or so she thought. Her sexuality had never entered into the equation because she had not needed it to. She was a Christian now and Christians do not participate in sexual activity outside of marriage, therefore, it was never given any consideration. Now as a married woman, she was totally confused. The old worldly thinking patterns took over because she allowed them to instead of heeding God's word which was not very specific toward sex in marriage; and she did not know any better. Alexis remembered that during a time of reconciliation, she and Kurt had prayed a prayer for God to search their hearts to see if there was any evil in them and then lead them in the way everlasting. Was God honoring this prayer by allowing what was going on? Alexis knew God was too great for her to understand and it frustrated her sometimes.

Contributing to her confusion, was the disconcerting thought of being so close to God, yet enjoying sex; she had a hard time reconciling the two. It just seemed like it did not fit together, a mix match that was not from God; it would be years until this issue was illuminated in a sermon that made it clear to her. Sex was not a godly thing, it was a worldly thing, and the only reason it was considered holy was because of the sanctity of marriage.

In the first year of their marriage Alexis struggled with the emotional baggage of not being able to conceive a child, remembering the prayer about not getting pregnant, having a data bank of information about her husband she did not know what to do with and the old man being adjudicated guilty of sexual intercourse with his eight year old granddaughter. In addition, there was Kurt's new job, sexual talks during his sleep about other woman, the promotion of inappropriate sexual talk with Alexis that usually led to sex, and him revealing the fact that he use to get so turned on when he watched pornography with his ex-wife.

Wait a minute! Alexis remembered their talk when they were dating about being ashamed of the past things in their lives before Christ. Wasn't this one of them? Why was he now glamorizing pornography like it was a drug he had to have some more of? Why was she talking about the sexual experiences in her life prior to Christ? How did she get here? Because he wanted her to be there, she justified.

The talk about pornography and the sexual escapades with his ex wife became a topic Kurt would bring up often. Alexis did not know how to counteract this because the attempts she had made to do so, thus far, were to no avail and she was vulnerable to this type of programming. Her misconception about her role as a Christian wife, married to her lack of education about pornography provided the ingredients for the recipe called "disaster". He was addicted to pornography when they met and she was unaware of it because he tried to hide it. Routine normal sex became boring to him even when they took a couple days off and he was unable to ejaculate unless he had stimulation from pornography. Alexis felt as if she had all of a sudden been tossed into a dryer like a cat who could not compete with staying on all four feet as the drum tumbled around and around, not to mention the intensifying heat that would eventually kill the cat; a precipice she felt imprisoned by.

In contrast there were times when she would pray and God would answer her prayers almost immediately, making it obvious He was still near her. For awhile, she interpreted this to mean that God wanted her to keep trying to make the relationship work at least that was the way it seemed to her.

Occasionally Kurt apologized for his behavior, presenting her with a beautiful poem or note he wrote, and permutated into what appeared to be the sweetest man on the face of the planet subsidizing her uneducated hunch of split personality.

"Dear Alexis: I love you and you are not any of those things I said (i.e. "idiot", "stupid", "baby") sorry for that. I really want our lives to enhance each other and I want you to be happy again with your choice to marry me. See ya after work, Kurt."

Then Alexis would feel so loving toward him and so loved by him, that she would be sucked right back into an unhealthy relational pattern, unaware of the existing precedent established long before Kurt ever met her that dictated how he would act in this relationship. It bothered her that he rarely apologized for, or admitted specific things that started the fighting in the first place, only generalities like "I'm sorry I got so mad," or "Sorry I called you a name". This had nothing to do with the genesis of the difficulty from his insensitivity toward her, his over-reaction to something he thought she said or an angry display over something stupid like the jar of mayonnaise being in the cabinet instead of the fridge. But Alexis was satisfied for now, hopeful that baby steps were taken toward the realization of what created the conflicts to begin with. His blanket apologies were at least something. Some men never expressed regret for anything, she thought. Unsuspecting that the conflict would intensify throughout the course of their relationship, the same way a drug addict's dependence grows with every use, she became hopeful that the behavior invoking the request for forgiveness would eventually change and knew that with God all things were possible. This was her husband; she needed to respect him and try to show mercy and grace as God had done for her.

Kurt and Alexis were compatible in many ways and had a good time enjoying similar things. For instance, when they became engaged, it was October. They drove to the mountains of Tennessee to spend a week exploring and hiking, breathing in the cool fall air and bringing a bag of leaves home displaying beautiful colors of gold, red, yellow and light green. They both loved this area of the states and had talked about someday buying land and building a cabin there. Together they would sit and enjoy sipping coffee on a porch of a lodge after eating breakfast out; he seemed to like the slow pace as much as she did.

Later that day when they drove by an area with a huge meadow, where deer were grazing, he stopped so she could get out and watch them for a little while; she loved wildlife. Then after a few minutes, he blew the horn of the car over and over as he laughed scaring the deer off into the woods. This behavior was foreign to her but she allocated it to him just being a guy and failed to see it as abnormally immature or a desire to ruin that which brought her happiness or pleasure

When they browsed through a quiet country store, he made her feel that if there was anything she wanted, anything at all, he would get it for her. He referred to her as, "the most honest, loyal, Godly, heavenly minded, beautiful, sexy, loving and all around awesome woman he had ever met". She was drowning in the love she felt thanking God for bringing Kurt to her. She enjoyed being with him. For the first time in a long time, spending time with a guy was pleasurable.

So the trouble was often washed away by Kurt's efforts to win her back to a place where he could position her making her vulnerable again, prepping her to be the target for his abuse. After all, what fun would it be to shoot at a target that had fallen over? Kurt would continue to secure the target and stand it back up before he continued shooting. The holes in Alexis' heart caused by Kurt shooting erratically should have been enough evidence to her for a safety hazard warning, however, in her ignorance she pushed forward, rising to be aimed at and hit repeatedly.

On occasion, Saturday mornings were spent at a local coffee shop eating bagels and enjoying a slowly sipped cup of coffee, just the two of them. The difficulty in their marriage was contrasted by the easiness of just being together and sharing the moment, constantly flip flopping her negative thoughts about him. That was just the way marriage was, she thought, everyone told her so.

They were almost there and Alexis was looking forward to the "wake up call" caffeine gave her. Kurt parked the car and opened her door as he always did unless they were fighting, and then they began walking across the road toward the shop. There were tables outside on the sidewalk where people were sitting and enjoying their morning coffee in the fresh air. Just before they reached the sidewalk and were about to step up over the curb, Kurt pushed Alexis. She tripped and almost fell down; everyone looked over at her.

"Why did you do that?" She asked embarrassed and shook up from almost crashing into the concrete under her feet.

"Because you were walking too slow. There was a car coming."

"What? You feel that pushing me to the point of almost pushing me to the ground was ok, just because you thought I was walking too slow?" Alexis was eager to please her husband but did fight back. "I almost fell and everyone looked at me. I wasn't walking too slow." She defended, having no idea that he was speaking untruth on purpose in hopes that she would correct him providing the springboard he instinctively needed to launch his

68

captive rage which had absolutely nothing to do with her or their relationship.

They were now inside the shop and Kurt was angry that she expressed her dissatisfaction with him about pushing her. He told her he did not want any coffee, and went out to the car, much the same way a child would throw a tantrum, and then go stomping off to his or her room to sulk. Kurt had invoked a fear inside her that he was going to leave without her, but she stood in line waiting for coffee nonetheless, just wanting to be away from him, baffled at what had just transpired, trying to make sense out of it.

Circumstances like these were common in their marriage beginning with the first real fight preventing any true sense of trust from lasting more than a few days. To Alexis, it seemed as if Kurt could not stand it when they got along and did something on purpose to cause a fight or argument. "That's crazy!" She thought. "That would be insanity. It must be me; maybe I should have hurried up more across the road in front of that car."

Ah, the sweet smell of success! Kurt was becoming victorious at getting her to look inward at herself as the source of their problems because of the contradictory messages and the exposure to ambiguous situations he continually invented. To this end, he would wound her sense of identity, alter her self-perceptions, and create a person who was unsure of herself; someone who was subliminally regressing psychologically, making her more anxious to please him to stop the behavior that made her miserable. But how could that be? How could you take a mentally healthy person and be successful at molding them this way? Alexis was still clueless about torture and how it worked. She did not know she was in a contest with her tormentor who had to win the contest or he would die.

They were supposed to run several errands after the coffee shop but Kurt started driving home after she positioned herself in the passenger's seat bewildered and quiet somewhat surprised he had not left.

"Where are you going?" She asked.
"Home."
"Why? We planned to get a lot done."
"Oh well." He looked depressed as if he was the one who had just been pushed in front of people.

"I think you pushed me on purpose just to manipulate me and cause a fight. As a matter of fact, I think you try to manipulate me to try to make me feel stupid so you can feel better about yourself or superior." Alexis was frantically digging up knowledge she had of bullying behavior, because that is what it seemed to her he was doing.

"The only reason you are using the word manipulate, is because I said it."

"What?" She asked in disbelief. "Like I didn't know about the word before you came along, or the fact that you manipulate me. Who is the foolish one? You act like I don't know anything until you tell me, like how to act, how to respond, how to feel, how to speak."

"I manipulate to prove foolishness, not to get what I want." He stated.

"Your manipulation is a sickness; you do it so much you don't even know what manipulation is and what's real. Besides, the fact that you can manipulate someone does not prove foolishness. Virtually anyone can be manipulated by deceitful words or actions. If you really wanted to prove foolishness then you would have to give someone all of the absolute truth, and then if they still choose the stupid response or decision, then you could say they are foolish. You can't prove anything with smoke and mirrors except deception on the part of the one using them." All of this made sense to Alexis but it did not matter because before she finished he had started screaming obscenities at her.

She attempted to talk about the situation further, to explain how it made her feel when he pushed her. In her mind, she still thought she was dealing with someone who was capable of thinking in logical terms, but he just started screaming back in rage at her, claiming she didn't need to feel that way and had no reason to feel that way. He said she needed to walk faster calling her childish and self centered and asked what they were fighting about. This made her feel dead to him emotionally; he did not get it at all. It was like trying to reason adult issues with a two year old.

Once they were home, she got out and he took off in the car, backing up before she was even all the way out, not returning until the next day. His ability to easily walk away treating her like she was dispensable, leaving her to sit there in wonderment, made her feel as if he thought of her as garbage. She felt as if she could have

71

been anybody at all because if he could leave her so easily, he did not really love her.

When he finally came home the next day and walked in the house without any explanation of where he had been, he mockingly asked her if she enjoyed her time alone acting as if he had punished her with the absence of himself believing in his own mind that just his mere presence deserved applause; she ignored him. After awhile he became displeased with her not paying any attention to him and began to joke around like the day before had been nothing and she should just forget it. He asked her if she wanted to have sex. "No thanks", she replied. She continued to ignore him, keeping busy with things around the house.

"This is stupid. I'm ready to be done with fighting." He said as he walked up behind her, put his arms around her, and snuggled, still giving no explanation of where he was. For the first couple of years and until Alexis figured out his personality dynamics, this usually melted her back into the pliable liquid he needed her to be, because the choices were to either make up his way or continue in the misery; she usually opted to make up. Nothing was discussed or resolved, it was just over. Then they would enjoy the physical oneness of marriage and enjoy the rest of the day going out to eat, renting a movie, or doing some other form of recreation, until the next explosion of rage.

The next week, Kurt took her out to lunch, and then brought her back to work. "Bye, I love you, see you later." Alexis said as she walked back into the office. Kurt was in the parking lot standing next to his vehicle. They had been getting along for a few days now after the coffee house, pushing scene. Kurt was obviously staring at an attractive blonde who was getting into her vehicle a few parking spots away, as he answered Alexis, "I love you too," never even turning his head to look at Alexis as he spoke; this bothered her.

Later that night Alexis mentioned it to Kurt. "It was nice of you to tell the blonde in the parking lot today that you loved her." Alexis was using humor to try to communicate with Kurt about something that had been bugging her all day. Typically, Alexis did not approach things with much tack but just came right out and said them. Candy coating words was not her forte and at this point she was still unaware that Kurt purposely tried to make her jealous so he could project his emotions onto her.

"What are you talking about?" Kurt asked in immediate outrage.

"When you said good bye to me today, you never even looked my way but you were looking at the blonde in the parking lot."

Changes in Kurt's face and voice became apparent as he started walking into the living room. The frontal display projected anger, hate and detest at Alexis, as she had never seen it in real life. "I never even saw any blonde; I must have been looking at a car driving by. You are nuts! You have a jealousy problem." He tried to grab his own hair with both hands and pull it out. This was a strange behavior to Alexis who did not have the slightest indication about why he did it.

73

In the fourth year of their marriage, Alexis would be able to understand this scene because what was really taking place was that Kurt was extremely jealous of one of the males Alexis worked with because she had talked about him at lunch and instead of being honest with her about his emotions and insecurities which would include facing reality, something he was incapable of doing, he had to manipulate a scene in which she became jealous so he could turn it around and project his feelings onto her.

But at this point with her current level of understanding regarding their relationship, and only eighteen months into the marriage, all she wanted was an acknowledgement that Kurt thought the woman was attractive, and then an apology for staring, with reassurance that she was his only one. Alexis was unaware that Kurt was incapable of any of the above. What she received instead was a denial that he even did it, an accusation that she had a jealousy problem, and disgorged rage.

Kurt tried to make her feel as if she was abnormal in some sort of way but Alexis knew most women thought the same way she did and all women notice when their man is obviously attracted to another woman. As a Christian, Alexis had high standards especially about protecting her marriage and thought that men who claimed to be Christians should have high standards too regarding women they thought were attractive. There was a point at which noticing became wrong if it passed a certain amount of time; a point where it became staring, lusting.

"Kurt, there was no one else in the parking lot except the two of you and that baloney about looking at a car driving by…"Alexis said as she followed him making the situation worse. She despised unreality and thought he should just fess up before he messed up.

He picked up the TV remote and smashed it against the coffee table leaving an indent as he grabbed his keys and left slamming the garage door down on the way out like he intended to break it; she ran after him out the front door.

"Where are you going?"
"Away from you. You need help."
Confrontations like this made Alexis feel like the joy of life had been withdrawn out of her soul with a vacuum much the same way a baby is ripped and pulled from its life-supporting environment in an abortion. Fighting in this way, unable to talk about anything, almost incapacitated her to the point where she would just sit on the sofa crying and stare at the wall. She did not want to live that way and would have never taken the first step toward marriage if she knew this was how it would be. It was worse than her first marriage where neither of them were Christians.

The swine face apparition popped up from the depths of the sea of data her mind stored. It was too late; she was already married to him. She prayed that good would come from this and committed to make the best of a bad situation because divorce was not an option. She collapsed in tears at the thought that God was trying to warn her to stay away from Kurt by revealing the swine image to her that had worked in the past; she had taken notice of it, but not submitted to it in faith, not committed it to memory as a permanent hedge.

But what was it about Kurt that allowed him to curtail the red flags flying in Alexis' head about him in the beginning and skirt around God's powerful presence in her life giving him access to her? The periphery of her understanding was lacking. The only survival method Alexis came up with was turning to the Lord in prayer never forgetting Him and reading His word on a continual basis. It was here she would find guidance, strength, and a mirror for her own sin, which would invoke repentance leading to life.

The desire to be what Kurt wanted was very strong because she was ready and willing to be submissive as a wife and willing to please her husband to make this marriage a success, telling him that she was going to learn how to love him in spite of himself. She would not be involved in, or drag her kids through, another divorce, it just would not happen. God hates divorce! Therefore, the desire to learn how to love Kurt grew in its intensity as well as the hunger to make this union work in defiance of evil's intent.

Alexis knew that Satan did not want them to be victorious and she considered it her job to provide the disappointment. She focused on scriptures like the one in first Corinthians that talks about the fact that you will have more trouble married than single, and Romans eight where it states that the Lord will cause all things to work together for good to those who love Him. But it says if you love the Lord, you will obey His commands, and one command she thought of was, "a servant of the Lord must not quarrel"; she was guilty. So during her prayer time she would ask for forgiveness for the way she argued with Kurt and any other sin she could think of that she had committed. Over time, she became skilled in not arguing with him, not allowing him to engage her in a sparing match, although he occasionally caught her off guard.

Her desire to please God was still there, but her desire to please her husband had overgrown it like vines on the side of a cobblestone building in Ireland whereby no visible sign of the stone could be seen behind the green leaves. This was one of the reasons she did not want to get re-married to begin with, explaining to a friend years before. She knew herself well, and knew that if she did marry, she would want to make her husband happy. She was fully aware of the scripture in first Corinthians that talks about women who are unmarried desire to please the Lord, but women who are married desire to please their husband. In consideration of what the Lord had done for her and how He had blessed her life, it was inconceivable to her that she would ever allow herself to want to please a man more than the Lord she so dearly loved; knowing it would be her downfall and seeing it coming a mile away. Even so, once she had a taste of the possibility that the feeling she had with God could be reproduced in the flesh through marriage, she was completely caught: hook, line and sinker.

Here she was in the exact place she had feared and had even spoken out loud. Why did she not keep it to herself? When would she learn to keep her mouth shut? Did Satan hear her? Was he now aware of her weakness? Had she revealed to him the susceptibility she knew she possessed that he could use to try to get her away from the Lord or get her to lose her faith in the Lord? After all, that was his mission, was it not, to get each Christian to lose their faith and trust in God? Is this why God tells us to be slow to speak? What about the scripture that says that nothing can separate us from the Lord? Sorting it out exhausted her.

Eighteen months after their marriage, Alexis found herself in a precarious position, especially spiritually. She did not like the way their lives were going and could feel the strain of the spirit against the flesh. It was obvious to her that Kurt was not interested in helping her draw close to God, but was attempting to lead her and the children away from God. Two years ago, she would have never believed that one day she would be married to a man who would be successful at bringing beer and pornography into her home. However, here she was, sitting with her husband, drinking a beer and watching pornography on her television. The children were with their father and she never allowed this activity when they were in the house.

In her mixed up sexuality, it turned her on to think that watching a porno flick with her husband revved up his engine toward her. In other words, it turned her on, to turn him on. She could take or leave the movie, but if you separated the flesh from the spirit, Alexis could confess that sex was something she really enjoyed and watching people having sex was stimulating to her. Statistics proved she was not the minority but part of the majority. Sex with Kurt was the best she had ever known in her life, better than she had ever heard or read about. Even outside of sex, just the way he kissed her, or caressed her shoulder, was as if he had been given covert operation information for melting her heart. He was extremely skilled in the way he touched her, sexually and non-sexually. Although she would admit, sex with him never felt like "making love" not even once including the first time. It was more like she was on the set of a porno flick and some important element was missing…it was empty of emotional involvement. Her mind flashed back to the prayer of finding any evil in her heart and then leading her in the way everlasting. Was this all part of it?

One complaint most women had of their husbands was that they were not affectionate enough. Kurt was very affectionate and in fact, he was so good at it, she thought he should conduct classes for other men, whose wives did not enjoy sex. He could have made the most frigid woman want to engage in a love session. He knew she felt this way; she told him all the time. He had learned what she liked physically and had perfected it; he had to, it was part of the game so that he could use it against her to his advantage when they were fighting. He would withhold all forms of affection from her like he was punishing her. In her innocence, not realizing the manipulation taking place, she was vulnerable to this torture tactic.

Once the talk about Alexis having sex with other men and pornography viewing had started, Kurt never had a problem again with ejaculation. She prided herself on the way her husband longed for her physically, enjoyed the joint union of sex constantly, and seemed to be totally sexually fulfilled by her. He would brag about their sex life in generalities and how happy he was to his friends.

At the same time, the conflict of God's will for her life in contrast to this activity never ceased to cause Alexis inner turmoil. After they shared a beer, watched a movie, participated in sex, and he fell asleep, Alexis would lay awake feeling physically fulfilled, but emotionally and spiritually empty. She felt like an actress in a play, not acting out of her free will, but because she had signed a contract to do so. She would always pray to God afterward, begging for forgiveness and stating her fears to Him: protecting her daughter and losing her husband.

Slowly it became apparent to her that Kurt needed pornography. Approaching the subject always caused a fight. He would argue and say he was not addicted to it and on occasion he would burn the last movie they bought just to prove it but then would make comments that sex was going to be boring without it. Then after a couple months, he would buy a new one. One time, Alexis was responsible for suggesting they stop to get one as they were out one night, because she knew how happy it made him and she was addicted to the way he acted toward her when they participated in watching pornography not really knowing what else to do. Without it, things were not quite the same. Also, protecting her daughter was a constant subconscious effort. In addition to this, sometimes she just became weary of fighting with him.

She had never studied the subject of pornography or its effects, and it had been at least fourteen years since she had seen or read any of it, but she suspected it was not a good thing even though she was confused about it. The topic was almost never discussed from the pulpit or in general, or by anyone she knew in the church. When it was mentioned from the pulpit, it was approached superficially, not in depth. Therefore, questions in her mind jockeyed for position. Questions like: is it ok as long as it is in the privacy of your own home, and both parties confer to watch it? She reflected on the way that Kurt seemed to go into a trance during viewing pornography, almost like he was sleep walking and any attempt to wake him up would disturb an essential balance. This was curious to her and a little scary; she just did not know any better.

The fact was that the people on the television screen were not married, and sometimes they had more than one partner; therefore, she concluded from those two facts alone that viewing the pornographic material was an ungodly activity, not to mention the objectification of women in general and all the other issues involved. Therefore, Alexis would pray to God that her husband's need to watch pornography would decrease or disappear altogether, or that the feelings generated by watching the pornography would be magically transformed by the emotions of love she thought he felt toward her. She would pray that he would hear a sermon on the radio, or someone would come into his life that would educate him on the subject and ask God to forgive her and Kurt and beg God to make robes from her rags. She was hopeful that this would somehow work together for good, acknowledging now that she should not have ever married Kurt in the first place, she hadn't given herself enough time to get to know him but she was anticipative that God could make beauty from ashes; divorce was not an option.

Part of her justification of the whole matter was that maybe this was the way Kurt would heal. To achieve intimacy with someone who was willing to walk down a road with him just a little away from God so that certain things would be revealed to him and God could work in him. Healing rarely comes without some sort of intimacy. There was only one thing wrong with that plan: it had a faulty premise; therefore, it also had a flawed outcome. Someone can never be pleasing to God by walking away from Him. If they are going in the wrong direction to begin with, they will never reach their destination and all the intentions in the world will not assure their arrival; they must change their course.

Alexis never stopped talking with God about the whole matter and asked Him for wisdom. The thought crossed her mind that in order to build a sidewalk fifteen feet away from a road, the lovely grassy area would have to defiled for a short period of time in order to get to where the sidewalk would be laid. Once the sidewalk was built, the grassy area could be restored, thereby making the final result better than the original creation, never giving indication that the grassy area was ever destroyed. Kind of the same way Christ took on the sins of the whole world while he was on the cross however, the result was our ability to be forgiven of sins. Without this shedding of blood, we would have no forgiveness.

She was of the opinion that she needed to be the defiled grassy area for a short period of time so that the sidewalk could be built and believed with all her heart that this was her ministry, an intrinsic assignment in light of her Christianity. In time, she would realize that this thought would also yield a faulty conclusion, due to its erroneous premise. The truth was that Christ was sinless and God would never desire us to sin, in order to achieve a godly outcome in any instance. His love is not indiscriminate, killing good things in our lives along with the bad like peroxide destroying the good cells along with the bad cells in a wound.

Sexually, Kurt had one special area that really turned him on. It was one female and more than one male participating in sexual activity and these were the types of pornographic movies they would watch and this was the type of fantasy talk he liked. He had told Alexis that most women can be talked into this sort of activity easily, making her think it was true. How was she to know otherwise? These manipulating words caused her to think that perhaps if she did not do what he liked, he would get it elsewhere.

Strictly sexually and naturally speaking Alexis knew that part of her could have been one of those women in the town of Corinth, where sexual immorality was running rampant, participating in orgies and the like. The natural man receives not the things of the spirit of God for they are foolishness to him; neither can he know them because they are spiritually discerned. The thought of more than one man trying to physically please her was, sexually speaking, a turn on for her also. Just as to a man, the most common sexual fantasy is to have more than one woman trying to physically please him.

However, she could not separate the flesh from the spirit and experienced the constant nagging of the Lord's will in her mind, and two years into the marriage, Alexis educated herself extensively regarding the affects of pornography on the human brain and society in general. The providence of God had made certain she heard a sermon on the radio about it, advertising a video and audiocassette. The Lord so patiently waits for this unmistakable turning.

What she learned about pornography scared her to the decision of deleting this activity from her life forever, and invoked a time of heavy repentance. If it had been back in Bible days, she would have been sitting in sack cloth and ashes. Her decision made Kurt angry and he berated her for it. She tried to educate him to get him to see that it was wrong, and convince him he had a sexual addiction problem originating all the way back to when he was ten years old when he first started viewing pornography and masturbating to it. She was never successful in this endeavor. One day after hearing a sermon at church about it, he would agree that it was not appropriate, but the next week, he would act as if he never agreed it was wrong in the first place, insisting that she stop trying to educate him about it. In one instance, yelling, "Stop talking to me about pornography!"

During an argument about it one time, she suggested he had actually never given pornography up when he became a Christian and he responded by accusing her of looking through his dresser drawers back at his apartment when he was single and they first started dating. She had never done that so he was telling on himself.

As she continued to study this subject, she noticed that the men who were being arrested for sexual crimes had a look about them; their eyes gave them away. Being addicted to pornography manifested itself into a specific look in the eyes of men and she became cognitively able to pick it out of a crowd the more she researched the subject and the more she studied Kurt. She was certain that if you interviewed the men that had the look, all of them would tell you they were addicted to pornography.

Kurt had this appearance about him and she had not noticed it before; it scared her. The more she studied, the more she was convinced that pornography was ruining society as a whole and it infuriated her. It reduced men to dogs in heat, going around wanting to hump everything. Their perceptions and judgments were skewed rendering them incapable of realistic organized thinking; delusion was their reality.

Unbeknownst to Alexis, Kurt didn't just have a temporary fascination with pornography as a man might have while between relationships, he was addicted to it and had an extensive past with his ex wife not only watching pornographic movies, but actually playing them out, participating in sexual escapades to the point where he said they had a library of such pornographic movies, and a variation of people they actually had sex with in threesomes and foursomes across town. What Alexis had learned about pornography addiction was that some men had addictive personalities and some did not. The ones who were in the percentage of having addictive personalities would find it very difficult, once involved in pornography, to turn away from it even if they entered a relationship.

Early on in their friendship, Kurt told Alexis he had done some things in his past that he was not proud of, sexual things with other people, but had not divulged the extent to which this was true. Likewise, Alexis had revealed to Kurt that she too had done some things in her past, before becoming a Christian, that she was ashamed of. Although she had never had anything but traditional sex: one man, one woman, she revealed to Kurt that she had cheated on her husband in two different affairs, and remembers the night she told him, because he kissed her very passionately after she said it. She figured that he was just glad to find someone that also had things in their past that they were embarrassed by, and she summed it up to an emotional connection. She was now realizing that he was sexually excited when she talked about being with another man and in his perversion this turned him on and that was the reason he had kissed her so passionately.

On occasion, Kurt said he and his ex wife would decide that sex with other people was destroying their marriage, acknowledging it was wrong and would quit for a while; however, they would always go back to it. He encouraged his ex wife to have boyfriends and to take pictures of her sexual escapades so he could see them, but then he complained to Alexis about how his ex cheated on him. The contradictions were so numerous, Alexis was coming to the point where she did not know who Kurt really was.

This was the reason Kurt had gone forward that time at church stating he was struggling with something. A couple he knew was soliciting him to be the third party in their sexual adventure and he was tempted to do it.

Before Alexis' educational awakening about pornography, and at the summit of Sin Mountain, Kurt had encouraged her to sleep with a man at her work who had started flirting with her and Kurt's sexual engine really intensified when they spoke about it. This was a strange thing to Alexis. In the past, before she became a Christian, while cheating on her husband, she deceived him; had to be discreet so that she would not be found out. Now she was married to a man who was encouraging her to sleep with someone else, even trying to get her to do it in front of him.

Was it coincidence that this man presented at the perfect time, was drop dead gorgeous and ten years younger than Alexis? What an ego boost; he was begging Alexis to have sex with him and it was tempting to say the least, but again, Alexis could not separate the flesh from the spirit of God living inside of her. She was honest with the guy and told him right up front about her husband encouraging her to sleep with him. She told the guy it was enticing to her, but she knew it was wrong and never felt that she was tempted beyond that point, although she did make stuff up to tell Kurt to turn him on during their love sessions. He encouraged Alexis to beg him for permission to sleep with the guy at work, stating that he really liked it when she did this. When she talked this way to Kurt, he could hardly control his sexual response.

In the course of many conversations with the man at work, some of which were spiritual, he said something to Alexis that resonated throughout her thinking process providing additional stimulus causing her to draw closer to God. The man, even though he was not a Christian, said that if he really loved someone, he certainly would not ever want to share her with someone else. As simple as it sounded, it convinced Alexis of her suspicions that Kurt's love was not pure and in addition, perverted.

Alexis wound up writing an apology letter to the man that included some scriptures from the thirteenth chapter of first Corinthians. She asked him to forgive her and they conversed about the text in the Bible that speaks about what love really is. She thanked the man and begged God for forgiveness for the way she often flirted with the person she knew Satan had provided at the right time and place, and for the way she spoke of it with her husband. The sin in her marriage was bad enough without this and she cringed at the thought of what could have been and rejoiced at the thought that it did not happen.

CHAPTER FOUR

Approximately two years after they were married, a fight perpetuated by Alexis' repeated attempts to educate her husband about the negative effects of pornography, her accusation that he had a lust problem which he called her jealousy problem, and her refusal to conform to the patterns he tried to establish, caused Kurt to leave the house in anger. She followed him outside, trying to talk to him, which only worked to make him angrier. He told her to leave him alone, in other words do not talk to him, which she admitted was something hard for her to do during times of conflict. She wanted to talk to resolve it, isn't that what you were suppose to do? He came at her, put both of his hands up against her shoulders, and pushed her down on the ground with such force that her feet came out from under her and she landed on her lower back and tailbone. They would be separated for almost a month.

During this time, in addition to constant repentance and prayer, Alexis began to strengthen, mentally, emotionally, and spiritually, vowing to become more pleasing to God than her husband regardless of the outcome. It would be another year before she would understand the full scope of the vicissitude she was experiencing. Nevertheless, slowly she reversed the ungodly decisions she had made over the past year and grew in wisdom as she examined the behavioral patterns and their resultant emotions in her marriage. The configuration of how Kurt would manipulate her became clearly visible and she would point this out to him, the calm observation in itself triggering his rage. She would eventually decide there was not much she could say that did not set his rage free; all she needed to do was be present. Increasingly he became transparent to her and she started changing her reactions to him.

She gazed upon her lawn and noticed the damage there. The correlation between her life and her lawn was like a slap in the face on a bitter cold morning. Constantly using any opportunity to teach her children spiritual values, she walked them around the yard explaining that the lawn was a representation of her life since she had allowed Kurt to influence her in a sinful way, participating in arguing and such. She did not go into detail with them about all the sins she had committed. She explained to them that this is what happened to her lawn of life when she let sin in; it permeated her life and caused damage.

Alexis prayed for decreased exposure to Kurt for her and the children, not really knowing what else to do. God honored that prayer with a new job for Kurt where he worked many hours. All in all, during four years of marriage, Kurt would have five different jobs.

One of the difficulties of developing a healthy relationship with Kurt had been the fact that there was never any conflict resolution. All Kurt needed was time to forget about whatever it was that started a fight in the first place, and then he became weary of the argument and desired to get back together. Or, he would just expect her to conform to his way of operation. Alexis on the other hand, knew that time did not change anything for her if the issue was not resolved. If three weeks passed without verbal communication of the problem, the original dispute still existed. Time did not solve it, talking about it and coming to some logical conclusion solved it or agreeing to disagree and moving on. She also knew that it was unfair for someone to assume their perspective was the only one and expect a kowtow from the other party.

Secondly, having a conversation with Kurt was all but impossible. He would claim that things were said that were not said, and claim that what was said never was. It was exhausting and unless you tape recorded the whole thing and played it back for him, you would never convince him otherwise.

During the time they were split up, he called her one morning to ask if they could talk when she was done with church services; she agreed to meet him. They met in a parking lot and the conversation became heated very quickly. He denied everything she accused him of including lusting after other women.

Even though Kurt had encouraged her to sleep with the man at her work, and despite the fact that she had apologized to the guy months ago and had told Kurt she had done so, during their conversation Kurt reached into the car window at her cell phone and said, "I know you've been calling him. Give me your phone, I want to check it." Alexis did not know what to say and just stared at him like he had two heads. She grabbed the phone away from him and left him standing in the parking lot as she drove off.

The red flagged data went into the bank: here was a man who was accusing her of having a jealousy problem, yet now he was jealous himself, after encouraging her to sleep with the man. It did not make much sense to her and was so contradictory. She thought about the split personality thing again, wondering if he was two people inside of one.

He called her on the cell phone. She told him the conversation was going nowhere and that he was incapable of talking anything out and hung up. He followed her all the way to the house, and eventually changed his tone when he realized she was not going to budge, telling her he wanted her back, that he wanted them to get back together and that he was sorry. He told her things that softened her enough to consider letting him come back. She was still in the atmosphere of giving him the benefit of the doubt for being genuine when it came to his apologies. Months down the road though he would deny that he ever said he wanted her back.

Then, something happened the next night that cinched the "getting back together" deal. Alexis did not know if it was her imagination, or a sign of some sort, however, it seemed that every time she and Kurt separated, something would transpire that caused them to get back together. In error, she assigned this as a sign from God that he wanted her to keep trying. However, God is not the God of confusion her conscious would tell her.

An escapee from the jail was loose and wandering around in the woods by her house. Helicopters were flying overhead and the kids were petrified. Alexis had always felt safer when Kurt was there; the kids did too, and wanted her to call him. She had done a decent job at portraying Kurt in a positive light to the children and making justifications for his bad behavior when it happened in front of them. In addition, her thinking at the time was still that divorcing Kurt was not an option because of her religion. She knew it was a matter of time before they got back together. So Alexis made the call,

"Hey, what are you doing?"
"Getting ready for bed; what do you want?"
"I need you to come to the house for the night. There is some escapee wandering around in the woods and we are scared."

"Is there sex in it for me?"
"I suppose. After all, we are still married. Hurry."
Kurt arrived there twenty-five minutes later and after the kids went to bed and fell asleep, him and Alexis went to bed and had sex.

Alexis had come down with a urinary tract infection during the time they were split up and had spent almost three days in bed without much movement. This caused pain in her back and it felt like something needed to click in it, but she had not visited the physician yet.

During sex that night, Alexis thought Kurt was being rough, almost like he was trying to punish her or hurt her on purpose through sex. Surely this was not the case she thought in the back of her mind. She did not like the way he was treating her and at one point she asked him to be a little easier as her back felt as if it would break under the pressure, then there was a sharp pain. She tried to find a position that did not hurt so much. Finally, he was done and she was relieved, however, in great discomfort. This evening together prompted their reunion the next day.

One of the stipulations of getting back together was marital counseling. There was no way she would allow him to come back unless he agreed to participate in counseling. He agreed. They started immediately seeing a Christian counselor recommended by the church. Although the counselor was highly recommended, he was not credentialed in diagnosing psychosis.

She poured out the whole story and they wound up arguing in front of the counselor on the first session. The counselor said he was glad for the mishap so he could witness the dynamics of their problems. "If this is how you are communicating, I can see why you have difficulty." He said.

It was determined through counseling that adultery had already taken place in their marriage due to the fantasy talk and pornography. The counselor told Alexis that if Kurt had not yet thought about sexually molesting her daughter that he eventually would because men who are addicted to pornography generally go on to take advantage of younger and younger females, especially pre-puberty girls. He explained that a scriptural basis for divorce existed; it was like he was giving her an "out" if she wanted it. Also ascertained through counseling was the fact that Kurt had serious anger issues he needed to deal with; anger toward women usually accompanied a sexual addiction. This anger, when it occurred, totally shut Alexis down, emotionally, and mentally; it was not her nature to communicate with anger.

Overall, the majority of the arrows were pointed at Kurt but he refused to see himself as the target, so when the counselor requested to see Alexis alone, Kurt arrogantly insinuated it was because she was the cause of their problems. Alexis was dumbfounded that he could actually convince himself of this.

During that session, the counselor asked Alexis a question: "If you are the totality of Kurt's misery as he has told you, then why does he stay with you?" This would be a question she would use in future arguments with Kurt when he propounded she was the reason they had marital trouble. It shut him up for a short period hinting that anyone who stayed with someone they claimed was the totality of their misery, was insane. The counselor also asked Alexis in a round about way, "Why are you with this person?"

Even considering the observations that came out through counseling, Alexis was still willing to try to make this marriage work, especially because of her religion that said God hates divorce! In times past, things might have been different, but now she was a Christian. Christians did not sell out of difficulty but embraced it, and reconciled relationships as Christ, their example, had done.

After eight or nine sessions, a mutual decision was made by Kurt and Alexis to stop counseling for the moment and try to make the marriage work on their own. It was expensive and not effective enough in view of the cost. In addition, Alexis had some decisions to make regarding her back pain, which was a constant reminder to her of that night she called Kurt to come back to the house. Had she interpreted the sign wrong?

Without positive results from five months of physical therapy, medication, and an MRI, her physician suggested surgery.

The imaging showed a bulging disc in her lower back so bad that the surgeon did not know how she was walking. In spite of the pain, Alexis had managed to continue working full time but she had progressed to the highest possible level through self-management without surgery, which meant she would still have constant pain and would not be able to run again. The neurosurgeon advised she was too young to be in pain and have her function limited for the rest of her life and explained exactly what he would do if in fact she chose to have surgery. She felt very assured of his competence.

The surgery was scheduled for two days before Christmas and Alexis' mother was flying in to help with the recovery period. She would cook, clean, and look after the kids if they needed it. It would be a nice time of visiting since they had not seen each other for over a year. Alexis took two weeks off from work and the kids were out of school.

Kurt had been very supportive through this time and it made Alexis glad she was still trying to make their marriage work. In the early morning of the day of surgery, he drove her to the hospital, helped her check in, and sat with her for the long wait in the pre-op holding area. They watched television and talked about everything non-substantial that you could think of. He had sex on his mind as he always did and wanted her to show him herself behind the curtain. She found his thoughts about sex to be incredibly immature and inappropriate at times and would occasionally make mention of such. These observations would be met with comments back to her about being a "prude" or "no fun" anymore. Alexis would then let it go; it was not worth the altercation and his words did not sting as bad as they use to. From this point forward, she began to ignore most of his ridicule attempts noting them as manipulation mines in a field for her to walk across.

When it was time for Alexis to be wheeled in for anesthesia, she was separated from Kurt and started to cry. This was her first surgery since her tonsils were taken out when she was two years old. She was scared especially in light of the contents in her data bank that she was still trying to classify. The anesthesiologist spoke with her briefly, and then her memory went on vacation until she woke up.

"Come on, Alexis, it is time to wake up." Alexis could hear the voice, but could not see the voice, which sounded aggravated, as if it had been trying to wake her up for an extended period of time. Slowly she realized her eyes were closed and opened them but only for a moment before she closed them again. Her eyes would remain closed while the hospital employees wheeled her up to her room. She could hear everything that was going on and hear her husband's voice following the entourage.

She did not feel like moving or breathing. Why did she feel so bad she wondered? The doctor explained that the surgery, which was scheduled to take thirty minutes, took two and a half hours instead. The piece of the disc that he removed did not slacken the nerve root. This would leave her in virtually the same state she was in before surgery. The neurosurgeon then explored the area below the disc and found an old injury that had become calcified and he had to pick and scrap the calcification out bit by bit. She had told him that the pain was radiating from an area lower than where he showed her the herniated disc was one time in his office before the surgery was scheduled; he remembered this. After the calcification was removed, the nerve root slackened considerably and the surgery would be successful in fixing Alexis' pain and limited function. It would take Alexis sixteen hours to fully come out of anesthesia, as she did not have a lot of body fat and therefore, the medication permeated her muscle where it would remain for awhile.

During the time that Kurt was waiting for Alexis to come out of surgery, he became scared. It was taking five times as long as what they told him it would take. After she was awake and speaking the next morning, he presented her with the letter he had written the day before while she was out.

In it he spoke of not liking the fact that he was all alone without her, a feeling of emptiness because he could not do anything but wait during surgery, and God had blessed him with their marriage. He also talked about the last six years being a treasure that will always last, which was puzzling to her because they had not been together for six years, only three, but she did not say anything about it knowing that guys were not real good at dates and times. He stated she had grown a lot, meaning in learning to deal with him. Was she making actual progress she wondered? Then at the end, he thanked her for sticking it out with him professing that women like her were hard to come by. Her heart melted and once again, she was assured that she was doing the right thing in trying to make their relationship work. What woman would not be moved by those words? Approximately a week after the surgery though, his inconsistent actions would once again result in a set back of her thoughts about him reducing her emotions to total disarray.

Alexis quickly recovered from her back surgery which was a huge success leaving her in a superior physically condition than before surgery, but the experience had changed her. The fact that she had a bad reaction to the anesthesia and had undergone something that had serious risks involved, including possible death, caused her to perceive life differently and think about things she had not previously considered with much effort. Like the question of whether or not her mother knew how much she appreciated her for the positive things she taught Alexis in her childhood.

Her mother had made some parenting decisions that were not beneficial, but there were three teachings that made all the difference in the world. Those three principles were: treat others the way you want to be treated, if you are going to do something do it right or do not do it at all, and there is a reason for everything. This formula was what Alexis subconsciously clung to, even if her performance of such was not always on target especially before she was converted to Christianity. Without these main concepts she would not have survived the dysfunctional environment she grew up in as well as she did.

She wrote her mother's funeral. This sounded strange to her mother and she explained it to her this way: "If you die before me, and I never speak these things to you, I will have regret in my heart for the rest of my life. Why do we wait until someone dies to speak things about them at their funeral that should be spoken when they are alive? Therefore, I have written several pages filled with explanations of where my appreciation of you comes from and the things that I am proud of you for." Her mother cried as she read it.

Alexis thought about life in general and being a Christian and how there is a cost involved with having your faith tested from time to time. You might endure the test but there is growth along the road and growth is typically painful. It prompted her to write a poem that one of her Christian friends did not seem to understand as well as one of her secular friends. This puzzled her because if anyone should understand the struggle between wanting to be with God in Heaven where there is no sorrow or tears, and wanting to stay on earth so that you could watch your kids grow or do something else you enjoyed, it was Christians.

Was it possible that some of them were not faithful Christians and therefore did not have any clue about the struggles between the spirit and the flesh? Was it possible that some of them were farther away from God than the secular friends she had? Not only was it possible, it was inevitable; Satan would make sure of it. Wide is the road and narrow is the gait and few be there that find it. She decided that one of the functions of the Holy Spirit was to be the operator of the scripture ticker tape inside her head.

Furthermore, did her kids understand how proud she was of them? She wrote them letters stating the facts thereof. The experience left her more appreciative of everything good God had bestowed upon her especially them. It made her more humble, better aware of her surroundings, and cognitive of the fact that life is short. She felt blessed to have had such a great surgeon who was intelligent enough to realize the removal of the protruding disc part had not solved the problem. What if this had not been the case?

She analyzed life; put it under a microscope, thought again about how she had walked away from God in sin with her husband, vowed to never do that again, regardless of whether or not her husband walked away from her.

Nine months after her back surgery, Alexis found herself in a meeting with her boss and her bosses' boss, where they presented her with a write up of bogus accusations against her. The television station where she worked for the past fifteen years had been taken over by another company two years ago. The first year was quiet and not many changes had been made. Recently though, employees were getting fired left and right, especially the ones who had been there awhile and who made descent money. One day they were there, the next day they were gone and no explanation of why was given to the remaining staff.

She would occasionally tell Kurt about some of the things that happened there and over the past few months, he had been encouraging her to quit her job, stating that they could manage without her salary. Later she would realize that he encouraged her to quit her job because this made her more helpless and he could manipulate her more in this position especially financially. He would later contradict himself and say that he never encouraged her to quit her job. Alexis had been employed since she was sixteen and the thought of not having the security of a job and relying on a man to support her intimidated her. On the other hand, she knew if an employer wanted to make someone miserable enough to leave a job that she was not going to win that fight; recently she felt as if she was their latest target.

If she had not undergone back surgery, and been provoked to think differently about life, she might have signed the notice being presented to her for the sake of argument and keeping her job that she had been at for ten years, conforming to their ways. However, she was not that woman anymore. So without further thought and with total disregard of the lack of security unemployment presents, she stood up to them. "I am not signing your little paper, because it is not true, and you can consider this my two weeks notice." Alexis arose and walked out the door.

LESSONS FROM THE LAWN – PART II

Alexis was now unexpectedly unemployed. It would be an adjustment seeing as how she planned on retiring from that particular job. But she had many hours of vacation time built up which would pay her for a few more months and decided to enjoy the time she had to be at home for a while without panic. Occasionally, she would bake cookies so that they were done when the kids came home from school and considered this a time of blessing. She realized how fatigued she had been working full time and taking care of a husband, two kids, and a home. For the first two months, she went

102

back to sleep every morning after everyone was off to his or her respective place. Ultimately, she felt caught up on her sleep and would only go back to bed a couple times a month.

With extra time on her hands, she decided to educate herself and do something about the lawn that was a mess by this time. For a season, Kurt had taken care of the lawn, or at least given the spurious impression that he was tending to it but with no barrier between them, weeds had been introduced to the beautiful, thick, green area that trusted its owner by its very innate composition to protect it from outside negative influences. The weeds seeped in slowly as to not be noticed until it was too late.

Kurt had not regularly applied chemicals that would maintain the yard's health or safeguard it from weeds and Alexis had not known any better. Sporadically, and in response to Alexis' complaining that the lawn was not doing so well, Kurt would spread a cheap bag of weed and feed just to shut her up. This method was ineffectual and the lack of proper maintenance finally prompted several episodes of tilling the ground in certain areas and laying down new sod.

The yard had become a point of contention more than once. When asked why he let the yard become unhealthy when in fact he claimed he could take care of it, Kurt would say, "That stupid yard; I don't care about it anymore. It's not important to me." To which Alexis would reply, "Since when? Why did you not say anything, I could have at least hired another yard company? Does it not matter to you that I would like to have a nice looking yard? And why do you drive by other people's yards and complain that their lawn looks awful, then say you do not care about our yard anymore?" Once again, there were too many contradictions with Kurt's behavior and speech to count.

Questions like this would usually send Kurt into a rage attack that would end up generating a huge fight. He would try to make Alexis feel guilty for desiring to have a nice looking yard the same way he tried to make her feel guilty for getting onto the kids about jumping around or rough housing on the furniture or running inside the house.

Alexis knew she was not abnormal for wanting to take care of the yard, or the things that God had blessed her with, like her furniture or teaching her children that outdoor play belonged outside. Others she knew desired nice lawns. In fact, the majority of the people she knew, earmarked time every weekend to take care of their lawns and gardens. In addition, many of her woman friends did not let their kids jump around on the furniture or run in the house and were stricter than she was.

She tried to figure him out and wondered if Kurt had a problem with giving up when something became too hard for him, declaring that it did not mean anything to him anymore, like when they were arguing and he would get to a certain point and just leave making her feel like he did not care about her anymore. Why was it so easy for him to walk away? It was an easy way out of being responsible, mature and resolving conflict. There was a quirk in him somewhere and there was something wrong; she just did not know what.

Making the equation even more difficult to solve, during the times they had to re plant the areas of grass, he would help her with the sod by taking his truck to get it, and helping her lay it down. It was always a fun time; they would turn on the radio and have cold drinks and turn it into a day outside, usually rewarding themselves with eating out afterward. It was a crazy thought but could someone actually enjoy destroying something just so they could rebuild it? Or build something for the purpose of destroying it? She dismissed the thought because it was nuts!

So here she was, all the time in the world to take care of the lawn herself and determined to make it look better, especially because of the correlation between her life and her lawn. She was not willing to let her life or her lawn go to shambles.

After several bags of weed and feed spread with a large plastic cup instead of the spreader, the yard took on a nice mosaic design of dark and light green. Kurt would shake his head and tell her she was going to kill the grass but at least she was doing something; she ignored him. Stagnation gives birth to death yet knowledge empowers us giving birth to desire, leading to life. The first step to getting the yard looking good was knowledge. The first step to getting her life back on track was acknowledging that it wasn't where it needed to be.

Lawn care was not a subject that particularly interested Alexis in the least, but she pursued it out of necessity and fear of losing her yard all together which was something she was not willing to do. Therefore, she asked questions at the garden centers, and of a neighbor whose yard looked healthy. She thought about the scripture that states wise people store up knowledge but the mouth of the foolish is near destruction; meaning simply that foolish people do not pursue knowledge.

As she studied the lawn, the spiritual parallel between her life and the yard with the dead spots and the weeds representing sin was devastating. As the awareness intensified, so did her desire to change the situation. In the beginning, she was a healthy yard but in spite of God's warning about him, she allowed Kurt to come into her life and he brought weeds and bugs, sort to speak. This was when the tucked away swine image lit up like a Christmas tree, resurfaced again, and advertised, through the appearance of the lawn, that she had not heeded God's warning. The thought overwhelmed her and fear of God's judgment married to her realization of a very bad decision allowing her to be deceived reproduced emotions associated with loss: grief, denial, anger, depression and acceptance. While becoming one together, she had taken on these bugs and weeds, which were negatively affecting her, spiritually, mentally, emotionally, physically, and financially causing dead spots and weeds in her as well as her yard. She was dumbfounded. God was using the yard to get her attention to understand what she had allowed to happen to her. She fell on the ground, put her hands to her face, started to cry and prayed: "God, please forgive me for not keeping the swine face warning as a hedge between Kurt and me.

Please reverse the damage I have created by being disobedient to you and forgive me for the sins that I have committed. Please help me to defeat sin as you have always defeated sin in history and protect me and the kids from it and its destruction. Your will is that none should perish but that all should find ever lasting life. Dear God, please take my rags and make them robes, please take my dismissal of the swine face and turn it into blessings. Please forgive me for my disobedience to you and your warning. I am so sorry for what I have done. In Jesus name, Amen."

Throughout the following days, and with words spoken out loud, she reasoned with God, "God, it was not like I totally disobeyed you. I really thought Kurt had changed, that the swine image was not a representation of who he was anymore. Please have mercy on me for allowing myself to be deceived and help me to have the wisdom I need to get through this situation." She wondered why God would have allowed her to marry such a one as this; couldn't he have just zapped her in the head or something?

One day, not too long after quitting her job, the local newspaper had a short clip about lawn care; it printed a number to call for further questions. Alexis called the number and spoke with a woman who was from the University who was an expert on lawn care and weeds offering advice and a brochure for St. Augustine grass care. By this time, a very resilient weed from the neighbor's yard, called crab grass, had permeated one whole side of her house and was quickly spreading throughout the back yard. Unfortunately, the entire east side of the yard, as well as part of the back, would be choked out by this hardy weed and have to be tilled up for a second time, and re planted. It made looking at her own sin all the more difficult as she realized that she had allowed herself to be carried away by her own lusts and desires in the very beginning with Kurt. Some people called it falling in love.

Crab grass, she learned, re-seeds itself even after winter has killed it off. It is truly amazing, killing and choking everything in its path as it gets stronger and grows rapidly across a yard like carpet being unrolled onto a floor even in adverse conditions. Sounded like Kurt and the sin he promoted. An aggressive weed killer is needed to kill it off, and then a pre-emergent continually applied to weaken the seeds from germinating. The stronger weed killers though will also kill the St. Augustine grass; it would have been much easier to be diligent in the beginning, protecting the St. Augustine lawn from the bahia with some type of barrier ensuring that the two would never meet. The spiritual and physical parallels were endless.

On one of those days when they were getting along well, Kurt was working in the garage and Alexis in the yard, for whatever reason he suggested a place in town where she could buy the right chemicals for the yard to help her be successful in making it healthy again. He had known all this time but had not volunteered the information until now; she thought that was odd. It was almost as if he enjoyed watching her struggle to get the yard in good shape again. Why were there so many contradictions about him? The considerations exhausted her.

CHAPTER FIVE

During the time Alexis was unemployed, she focused on her life and her lawn with gusto; the results becoming perceptible to the eye, even her kids noticed. She would tell Kurt often how much she appreciated the fact that he was supporting the family; this was something that not every woman could claim. She tried to focus on the positive about their relationship, a strategy that is beneficial in all areas of life not just marriage.

It was now approximately three and a half years after their wedding. Alexis had made magnificent progress in her responses to Kurt; ignoring his attempts of manipulation the majority of the time, not speaking to him about anything substantial; however, not much had changed in relation to his explosive mannerisms. In spite of her effectual changes, which seemed to benefit only her in that she was not affected as much in the fallout of the detonation, he still managed to invoke a reaction out of her, that would allow him to rage. Without the ability to emotionally cripple her Alexis noticed that Kurt was depressed often, sleeping sometimes for hours or all day on the weekends. Even though what they had was not much of a marriage and more like rolling a heavy stone uphill that always rolled back down again, hope still trickled forth from Alexis' heart like a Montana tributary spring bubbling up from the ground on Mount Jefferson, near the Continental Divide in Montana's remote Centennial Valley, creating the headwater of the Missouri River in spite of the fact that it had over thirty seven hundred miles to travel to the Gulf of Mexico.

One of Alexis' major support areas was Christian music. There was one particular song by the Christian artist Steve Bell[4] that ministered to Alexis "…Yet a flower can endure the course of a storm, by bowing to the tempest's rage". Kurt made fun of this song and Alexis for liking it, trying to manipulate her in his sadistic way, attempting to conceal his fear that she likened him to the tempest's rage, but she was beyond allowing him to alter how she felt about the song and played it often. She felt as if he was upset that he could no longer break her, that she was finding ways to survive and endure in spite of his repeated attempts at torture and abuse.

Alexis had also begun nurturing the friendships she had and planned more activities with the kids alone, however one weekend, they took the kids together to a mall in a larger town close to where they lived. Alexis and Kurt had not been getting along very well that weekend. By now, almost guaranteed, they could not go an entire week without some difficulty and although Alexis had made progress in dealing with him, she still did not know the whole truth of the matter.

While the kids were walking around the mall, Kurt walked out to the car; Alexis followed trying to discuss an issue from earlier that day. Sometimes it seemed to her that he was refusing to resolve conflict purposely for some odd reason. If his life depended on it, he would not talk anything through. He was trying to ruin a fun day for the kids like a child who gets in trouble and then purposely destroys one of his or her own toys or better yet, someone else's toys. Alexis was very aware of the behavior, but had no clue what triggered it.

When they arrived at the vehicle, and opened the doors, they sat down and Alexis looked at him. The changes that appeared in Kurt's eyes when he was angry began to bother her to a point where she suspected demonic activity within him. During this loud discussion in the parking lot, which was embarrassing to Alexis, Kurt said something that was so preposterous Alexis knew he was lying. She stopped in mid sentence just staring at him in disbelief, "What? You just made that up." He did not know what to say; he was caught red handed.

At this point, Alexis correctly identified Kurt as a pathological liar, but she did not know why he would lie about something so stupid. Why did he feel it was necessary to do so? Had she dug into his psyche deep enough to a point where he involuntarily was revealing a glimpse into his sick mind that would enable her to figure out what was going on? Or was it her perception that was improving? In a way, she felt sorry for him because she realized that he would have to be off the mark considerably from normal to really believe what he said happened, or to make it up. Either way, he was delusional; there was a serious problem. If she had not pursued him and kept him talking would it have ever come out? She had suspected he had lied in the past but he was so good at it that she could never prove it.

She had always been fascinated with psychological studies and found movies that were considered psycho thrillers captivating;

however, they always left her thirsty for answers. Why did the killer feel it was necessary to kill? What mental pathway allowed him or her to commit the psychological error that was considered "abnormal behavior" by society? Why did people think that ten years in prison would be effective in changing the thought patterns of a sexual predator? How far back would you have to go to trace where the personality flaw had occurred? Was it one incident or a culmination of consistent abuses that would create a killer? What was the "real ratio for blame" between environmental surroundings versus chemical make up as being responsible for producing individuals who were not assets to society?

As usual, she prayed that evening, pouring her heart out to her God. She asked him something she had not prayed for before now and that was for God to reveal the truth about Kurt to her so that she could understand. The past few years felt like a journey of wandering in the dessert searching for the answer as to why she was there in the first place. Even though her need for food and water were being met, and she was getting to know the dessert very well, she was still growing weary and knew that if she stayed there, she would perish. Knowing the truth would provide her with strength to go on and perhaps illuminate a trail leading out of the desert.

Three months into her unemployment, and the day after the argument in the parking lot at the mall, she sat at the library in front of a computer she had used to access the Internet. Not knowing how else to proceed, she typed "pathological liar" into the search engine. Information about Narcissistic Personality Disorder (NPD) came up.

At first as she was reading, she wondered if she had been sent on a wild goose chase by the internet search engine. Whoever heard of NPD, and what does it have to do with lying? Then after a few paragraphs, she freaked out. The information she was reading described her marriage and her husband as if there had been a fly on the wall in every instant, each conversation, and all occurrences of their lives.

She looked around the library to check and see if anyone recognized the fright on her face as the words she read burned in her heart. Now she understood the genesis for their first argument which was sparked by her criticism of him resulting in his response of inappropriate rage. People with NPD cannot handle any form of criticism. Frankly, it seemed like all of their arguments came about whenever she criticized him, whether constructive or not, whether approached gently or not. And lately, she felt like Kurt was trying to destroy her and everything good in her life, another symptom of NPD. The reason he did this was because he envied her; she was everything he could not be, and of course the progression of envy leads to hate…he hated her.

She continued reading and learned that unless she provided emotional stability and comfort for him, virtually agreeing with everything all the time, she had no value in his eyes. That would explain why she felt devalued at the drop of a hat. She must have made Kurt feel uncomfortable often with her "let's embrace reality" way of living especially as she strengthened emotionally and mentally confronting him with aspects of himself that were

113

detrimental to their relationship. He must totally hate her, she thought.

Ten pages later, the evidence convinced her that this personality disorder was responsible for all of Kurt's behavior and her responses ruining their marriage. This was when the link between Kurt's eyes and Ivan's eyes connected in her brain. They were the same eyes, she was sure of it. How could that happen? Was demonic activity responsible? If so, how did it work? A demonic spirit needs a physical body to dwell in, in order to accomplish evil deeds, but could they leave one body at will and enter another one? How did they enter the person? Does the person they posses have to die in order for the spirit to go into someone else? Is evil always present within us and it is just a matter of cooperating with it? Would you have to cooperate with the demons in order for them to have dominion over you? Are there similar evil spirits that work in groups? Her Nancy Drew imagination blossomed with the possibilities. Ivan had set out to destroy her, but was unsuccessful in that endeavor. Now, there was a person who was attempting to accomplish that feat and he lived in her own house! Had the evil spirit left Ivan and come into her husband?

The web listed several books by different authors on Narcissistic Personality Disorder and that week she was at the bookstore purchasing all of them. Even though one of the books consisted of over seven hundred pages[5], it did not matter to her; in fourteen days, she had finished reading all three of them. The volumes worked only to substantiate her hypothesis about who Kurt

114

was. The truth was revealed, the prayer answered and she understood every dynamic about their relationship, she just did not know what to do with the information she had.

Therefore, it would remain a secret in her psyche where it stayed for six weeks. Not once in all her studying of psychology was NPD mentioned, nor had she ever heard anyone she knew speak about it. It was a hard pill to swallow, learning that the man you supposedly fell head over heels in love with, objectifies you to the point where you could be anyone, lies about almost everything, and has two selves where neither are really who he is. It was like discovering baked meringue for the first time setting your heart on it to be something substantial, poking at the tall lightly browned peaks not knowing they would crumble into a powdery substance exposing the emptiness inside, the nothingness that it was made of.

Because there was no-one she could talk to and she was not sure what she was going to do, she had to journal; she had to have some sort of "out" for expressing herself and her emotions.

Journal Entry

I wonder what you would do if I confronted you with the truth I know: that you purposely deceived me to get me to marry you before I could see the real you. That is the reason why you pushed for things to go so quickly; it was all part of your game. History shows you would probably deny it and flee the scene. First you might accuse me of the very things you are guilty of. You might return wanting to make up or coldly devalue me not expecting to

115

ever see me again. You've done both. I didn't know back then the things I know now. If I had, it might have been different. Although I knew enough to know something was not right in your head, before last month, I thought we just had a bad marriage. A fairly calm, happy person teamed up with a miserable, critical person prone to rage attacks. The classic of opposites attract, except it was skewed because you didn't show me the real you. If you had, there would have been no attraction for me. You are a very good actor. Really! You deserve an Oscar. What a tangled web you weave. What anger and betrayal you invoke in me, your permanent supply source. I'm suppose to supply you with constant admiration and approval while you vacillate between thinking I'm great and then the scum of the earth, all the while inappropriately entertaining sexual thoughts, perhaps carrying them out, of other women to use as female source supplies. What a deal! I say sarcastically. Now I know that all of the thoughts I developed about you over the years beginning after five months of marriage were right. What would you do if you knew that I knew you did in fact have inappropriate thoughts about my daughter? You would run and deny, deny and run. Are you blind? Don't you see the patterns over the years? Every time you are confronted with a truth about yourself, you deny and run. You are in total denial. It is always someone else's fault, never yours. Everyone else is the one who is crazy right? It can't be you. Everyone you have ever worked for is crazy, all the women you've been involved with are crazy, your family is crazy (well that's true actually), but don't you see the common denominator here? Part of me wants to write all the truth I suspected and now know without a doubt in a letter and present it to you even though I know you would deny it and become enraged. Part of me wants to run as fast as I can away from you and never look at, or speak to, you again. Part of me desires that you be judged for what you've thought, done and the path of lies that have paved the way for every road you have ever taken. The last part, a small part would like to see your mind healed from all of it because I know where it comes from and it is really not your fault. But that part is divided in two with half of each part struggling against the other. One believing you can overcome this and the other knowing you never will. Any left over parts are just confused. So I go back and forth from anger, betrayal and disgust to pity, acting a part in the play of our lives and hoping against all hope that you can grow and mature. I can't tell whether my discovery about and assumption of your obvious diagnosis last month has helped or hindered my ability to cope with you. It's new and so I'll have to wait and see. And I'm still undecided as to exactly what I'm going to do about it. Every single problem we have had in our marriage is related to this. Everything I have suspected, you are guilty of, and is part of this disorder. I'm sleepy now, exhausted is more like it, good night for now journal.

The next day she wrote in her journal the dream she had that night.

Journal Entry- Dream:

I heard whimpering in the bathroom. I walked in and found Kurt fully clothed in the bathtub which was full of water. He was

117

submerged but could still make whimpering crying noises. He had thick black tar all over his face and down his neck even over his eyes and mouth so that no skin could be seen on his face. I knew he was trying to hurt himself and at the same time not wanting to. I panicked, "What are you doing?" I screamed. He started to cry. I reached in the tub under his shoulder area and pulled him up to sit him up in the tub. I started to wipe the tar off his face and now instead of whimpering he was fully crying. Then the scene switched to being outside and I was looking for him around the house, it was not our house and there were a lot of people around but no-one seemed to even notice what was going on. Kurt left in his truck and screamed, "Stop trying to save me."

Alexis had not read anything in the three books about demonic activity, but during her research, the swine image from the restaurant scene became implicated as the place where Jesus had sent the demons and it all made sense to her. The pig face image that she had understood to be an indication of evil never crossed her mind as a place of demonic activity, only evil. Thinking about it made her feel stupid and unworthy of anything good because she knew the story out of the book of Mark. She had read it several times and should have known better and correlated the two. She suddenly felt like she was inside some real life size sadistic video game, where people were watching her to see if she would make it to the safety zone, and if she did, then she would get to move to the next level and live a little while longer. She cried, prayed, and fell on the floor in a pile of sorrow and shame, begging God to deliver her from the evil she had invited into her own home by not forever yielding to His pig face warning.

Kurt was unaware that he was a specimen in a laboratory study; it had not been planned out that way, just happened. The pieces to the puzzle started to fall into place as Alexis realized that Kurt was sadistic and evil, and his goal was to steal her joy, kill the good relationships she had including with her kids, and destroy everything good in her life. He could not help it, he had to do it; it was his way of survival. The prognosis for the disorder was not favorable because the entire foundation of the disorder was a denial of reality in general, which did not leave much to work with! It was not like Kurt was an alcoholic who could admit that he drank too much when he was sober.

She had two different reactions simultaneously to the information roving throughout her intellectual faculties. The first was pity because of what a person would have to endure as an infant or child to allow a personality disorder of this caliber to develop. The second reaction was that she would have to separate herself and her children from this person quickly; she did not have a choice. It was not safe or healthy to be around him.

Strategies for survival in a relationship with the narcissistic personality disordered were offered in the research material and surprisingly most of them were tactics she had already activated a year and a half ago during their separation. She focused on nurturing and maintaining her own friendships, making godly decisions

119

regardless of his reactions, minimizing her responses to his insults and degradations of her person while slowly decreasing the power and control he had over her. She did not talk with him about her life much; that would just give him information with which to use to control and manipulate her. Until she knew what she was going to do, she would stick to this plan and move forward.

The books on this subject were not light reading and one of the hardest things for Alexis was that the information invoked introspection for her own narcissistic tendencies. Everyone who takes care of themselves well is narcissistic to a degree because you have to love yourself to take care of yourself; however, what separates the disordered from the normal is the degree to which the traits are present and how many traits a person possesses. The listed criteria suggested a person needed five of the nine behaviors in order to be diagnosed as having narcissistic personality disorder. Alexis took a deep breath as she began to read. At the end of the list she surmised that she had been guilty a time or two in her youth of using people selfishly to achieve a specific goal for herself like the time when she was twelve and told her mother that she was going to her friend Bernadette's house when she was really going to see her boyfriend. She admitted that there were periods of time in her life when she had been extremely selfish, however, she had matured in these things and learned a few lessons along the way.

This was the only listed criterion she could even relate to. The others were so bizarre to her, as was Kurt himself. But even if she had displayed more than one of the listed criteria, the attestation

120

that she had it was contrary enough to deny the diagnosis in the first place. People who have Narcissistic Personality Disorder typically are not even willing to admit to any of the listed decisive factors. Kurt, as far as Alexis could determine, owned all of the nine criteria listed.

The books also taught that most people conclude in error, abnormal narcissism deals with people who love themselves too much. There is a huge difference between narcissistic personality disorder and being selfish, egotistical, or conceited. Stating someone loves his or her self does not describe narcissistic personality disorder at all. In fact, the image portrayed by the narcissistically disordered of being a happy, fun loving, do anything for you likable kind of person, is the opposite of whom they see themselves as. They see themselves as someone who deserves to be abandoned, punished and abused, but they try to cover that up with a superfluously positive personality which is very attractive to most women because they come across as exciting, outgoing and confident. In the end, they really do not believe they are either, for to endorse one, would mean abdication of the other, and they need both to survive.

It was all making sense to her; that is why Kurt continually started fights when things were going well. He had to prove to himself that he was right about the fact that he thought he deserved to be abandoned and punished; even though he had to maintain a sparkling image on the outside. In private, he had to act in a way that assured he was the awful person part of him thought he was. Boy, he must have been miserable, she thought, because she kept forgiving him, taking him back, not quitting, not giving up on their marriage, not abandoning him. He must have been exhausted trying to manipulate the scene he needed in order to exist.

Journal Entry

I've done research about various subjects, including the negative affects of pornography which are many, however, I was only spot checking for fires wasn't I? We went to marriage seminars, listened to sermons and went to marriage counseling where you said that I needed to go because you didn't have any problems. Remember that? This was all in the hopes of understanding you better so I could love you better. Then last month a helicopter was provided for me, which I believe was an answer to my prayer for the truth about you to be revealed. I feel very confident that the information I found is in fact the revealment I prayed for. I was flown in this helicopter over the spot fires which are actually one huge forest fire that never stops consuming land. I can see it from up above now, its hugeness. No fire fighter in his right mind would fight this fire. No matter how many fire fighters there are, they are unable to control this inferno, so they've all gone home and given up. It's a blow up on a class D fire with at least 100 acres of damage. It kills and destroys quickly before its victims know what hit them. Like the charcoaled deer who was standing there when the wind changed and it was consumed by fire before it could suck in enough air to jolt away, not knowing which direction to go, therefore helpless where it stood and burned to death. No, I won't be one of

122

them. I might have singe marks on me that will scar, but I'm up above, here in the helicopter, watching the wind, and the fire's direction before it goes there. It doesn't make the devastation any less painful to watch but the heat is not as intense up here. That's how I would describe life with you before the revealment: being in a forest fire getting burned, not sure where the next spot fire would pop up. It's intense and life threatening, for you desire to suck the breath right out of me by various subconscious methods. Before the helicopter came I felt as if I was being lowered into Mann Gulch at the Gates of the Mountains on August 5th, 1949, never to come out alive again. I think about all of the fighting in vain. It's never made a difference. It was a release for you, an opportunity for you to vent all of the feelings that you are incapable of acknowledging for yourself; an attempt to experience them by projecting them onto me.

While Alexis was sitting on the couch reading the longest book of the three for a second time around, Kurt walked by her and asked, "What are you reading?"

"Research material." She answered indifferently, not wanting to engage in a conversation about it yet, because she was not sure how to approach it. She thought to herself that she had the books out in the open on the coffee table for two weeks, certainly he would have seen them by now, and flipped through them.

To her disbelief, a few days later he picked up the longest book and began reading it. She did not say anything to him about it wanting to hold her breath; hopeful that maybe he would gain some knowledge about himself that would make it possible for him to become mentally healthy again. He made it to page one hundred, and then did not read any farther, making comments that it was getting redundant and sounded like his boss, or her.

"It was true!" She thought. "He would never admit to any of it." There it was in black and white, the words on the page alive in the air he was breathing, indisputably describing his behavior and the way his mind worked yet he still refused to see it. Or were his words a cover up because he knew the book described him in totality? You could never be sure with this disorder, which display of self they really believed at any given time; the ambiguities were endless, therefore you could never really know them because they did not ever know themselves.

Journal Entry

Before I found out the truth about you, it was like trying to put a puzzle together without the box top to see what the picture was. I think about the constant berating, the criticizing, the verbal abuse, the cussing and the name calling that you spit my way. You have to constantly prove to yourself that you can manipulate me, which in your mind proves that you are superior, except you fail to see when you are manipulated by others. I think about how you have trouble cooperating with anyone over an extended period of time because you mostly think about yourself. You are extremely insensitive and arrogant. I sometimes find it hard to believe that I actually put the puzzle together at all. No-one would believe me if I told them what the picture was. Part of me is satisfied because at least I have answers. I understand now why you do the things you do but I don't like it and I really don't like you. You make me sick. Remember that time you were staring at Pete and Priscilla and he was rubbing her back. You criticized the way he was doing it. I now know that at that moment you envied Pete because Priscilla was a primary supply source for you at the time. You envy, then you hate what you envy, a vicious cycle. You wanted to be Pete rubbing Priscilla's back and you criticized him because criticism is a cover up for you; you use it when you need it to manipulate. It's hard being me with you. It hurts knowing that you fantasize about other women; about being with them and more than likely have cheated on me; although you have made the comment that as soon as they got to know you, they'd be gone. You're right! Most times I am unsuccessful at de-personalizing this aspect of your personality. Part of you knows who you are, but that's not really who you are, and the part that thinks it knows the other part is not really you either. There is no you. You have no clue who you are because you or your needs and emotions were never taken seriously from the moment you were conceived. Your parents screamed at you from the beginning, angry that you were even made. Every basic need you had was met with contempt. There was anger, punishment, criticizing, you were made fun of when you were hurt physically or emotionally. You were treated worse than if you didn't exist, you were treated as if it was your fault that you did exist. There were broken promises repeatedly. Do they have any idea what this did to you? It makes me sick. So as a child who was treated with contempt in every aspect of the word, and not loved, in order to survive you had to convince yourself that you weren't bad which turned into the false, grandiose self, to cover up the part that knew you must be bad. Why else would you be treated that way? Neither part is really who you are and it is much more complicated than my simple sentence. Both parts of who you are that you have made up in your mind for survival are exaggerations. Who you really should have been was never developed and never will be. The early years is where that takes place and those years are gone forever. Part of me is scared that I have the answers. It is not good news. It is highly unlikely you will change or ever admit that you have this disorder. I quickly scramble to focus on whatever part of our relationship is good, trying not to think about the negative; trying to stay up in the helicopter and not become the charcoaled petrified deer.

Six weeks after her discovery of his disorder, Alexis would go back to work with Kurt after dinner so that he could finish up some things. With all the data from the three books running around in her head, she listened to Kurt as he blurted out something about the secretary, once again successful at catching her off guard to manipulate a scene he needed for his real life movie.

"I asked Loretta if she slept with Steve."

"What?" Alexis asked him in disbelief. This had nothing to do with what they were talking about.

"The guys were wanting me to ask Loretta if she slept with Steve."

"Why would a Christian man be speaking with a single woman he works with about who she is sleeping with?"

"____ off!" He always responded with profanity when Alexis tried to hold him accountable to Christianity and she received that evil look.

"Seriously, why would you ask her that?" She ignored the obscenity and was not as intimidated by his loudness as she had been in the past.

"Because the guys wanted to know." He yelled as he was working on something.

"If they wanted to know, why didn't you tell them to ask her?"

"I did not think about that, I'll do that next time." He said sarcastically.

Alexis was getting jealous about the whole thing now. He had caught her off guard again and they had been getting along for a little while with no major blowups and she was still emotionally attached to him because she had not yet come to the point of giving up on their relationship. Alexis would eventually become totally emotionally detached from him but for now she still cared whether or not there was another woman around. She had not come to the place where divorce was an option.

He kept on. "She said she did sleep with Steve, but she wishes she hadn't. The guys were also talking about her sleeping with Mike and having him and another guy over at her house to play cards. I wanted to know if it was true so I asked her."

"Kurt, I don't think you should be talking with any woman, especially a single woman you work with about whom they are sleeping with; it is inappropriate." Alexis was becoming angry, still not perfectly skilled regarding the tactics Kurt used to get to her, but aware of the fact that if the secretary was entertaining two men in her home at one time, it would turn Kurt on and was right up his alley. Because of his sexual addiction and perversion about being turned on by two guys with one woman, she knew he would automatically and uncontrollably be drawn to her.

The secretary at Kurt's place of employment had been there now for about eight months and Kurt described her as dumpy, nothing to be concerned with. Alexis knew from experience that if the secretary was the slightest bit attractive, Kurt would have to try to extract inappropriate attention from her; he did not have the self control needed to stop this behavior as a married man. Alexis had figured this out about Kurt on her own regarding women and the books verified it.

When Alexis met the secretary at the company Christmas party, she was baffled; her only consistent state since her relationship with Kurt began. The secretary was the direct opposite of how Kurt described her: petite, cute, and sexy. Why did he lie about her? Alexis thought about the conversations over the past four months regarding the secretary; they were bizarre to say the least. At the Christmas party, both the secretary and Kurt acted strangely around one another.

Alexis had cheated on her ex husband approximately ten years ago, but still remembered and was fully aware of the body language people used around someone they were having an affair with. She refused to steep that low in her thoughts, besides, she could not prove anything by speculation, but what she saw between Kurt and the secretary went into the data bank.

Once the secretary left the party, which was shortly after she met Alexis, Alexis calmly asked Kurt, "Why did you describe her as dumpy? She's not dumpy at all, she's cute." These words of course, prompted a rage attack by Kurt who became pugnacious and they left the party shortly thereafter. Kurt dropped Alexis off at home and left; he was gone for about three hours. She did not know where he was, although her mind suggested to her that he went to the secretary's house, which was only two miles from theirs as it turned out. Kurt had made a point to tell Alexis where the secretary lived as they were driving by one day, but she refused to exert any energy on checking up with the hint, and eventually would come to a place where she did not care anymore.

It was now three months after the Christmas party, they were at home and the issue of how Alexis thought it was inappropriate for Kurt to talk to the secretary about her sexual escapades had never been resolved and had resurfaced in conversation. Alexis was trying to get Kurt to see her perspective still hoping this was possible and that she could help him but she was getting nowhere with him and he just became mad. He locked her out of the house and laughed about it while she was in the garage in her pajamas and it took her twenty minutes to get him to unlock the door as she knocked repeatedly. Then he locked her out of the bedroom right before she was ready to go to bed. She asked him to at least give her a pillow and blanket so she could sleep on the couch but he wouldn't. The dam of information inside her that she had been trying to keep to herself busted and she began speaking through the bedroom door at him. She did not scream but spoke with clarity, firmness and in a normal volume. This is the first time since she read the books that she revealed to him she knew he had this personality disorder. She felt like a clinician in the relationship and felt sorry for him, like he needed to be rescued and she was the one who was going to do it. She wasn't giving up on the fact yet that maybe he would face reality about himself and they could make their marriage work. Unbelievably she still had hope.

"Kurt, the book is correct about your behavior. You do have narcissistic personality disorder and that is the reason you need to extract attention from most of the woman you are around. There is a whole list of them, Priscilla being one, and Jill, and Lori. I know all this; I've known for awhile." There was no sound coming from behind the door; Alexis continued.

"You don't like hearing the truth about situations and so you respond in rage to anything I say that is real. Don't you see the patterns in yourself? I do not have a jealousy problem, you are the one who is actually jealous, but you project that emotion onto me by

130

making sure you create situations in which I respond in jealousy. You also have a lust problem, a sexual addiction and you are a pathological liar. You have to make me out to be the one with the problems because you can never admit you have them. Don't you understand what is going on inside yourself? It is all true."

When she finished, she laid down on the couch. In her hopelessly romantic fantasy mind, she pictured him coming out of the bedroom in tears, asking her to help him, telling her he loved her. Instead, he came out and got a drink of water with a look on his face that scared her. When he did this, she went into the bedroom and locked the door. He laughed and became antagonistic toward her yelling things from the couch through the door. She got up, opened the door and responded as she stood under the doorframe. He said something else, then she abandoned her calm demeanor and went over to the couch where he was laying and stood in front of the couch.

"The truth of the whole matter is that it was inappropriate for you to speak to Loretta about who she slept with, that's all I was trying to get you to see, but it turned you on to do so, so you did it. And this baloney about describing her as dumpy was a cover up; you did that on purpose so that I would not know you were attracted to her. Your whole life is a cover up. You are incapable of acknowledging a woman is attractive stopping your thoughts there. You cannot stop yourself from this behavior because you have a sexual addiction problem. It also turned you on to think that she would sleep with two men at the same time, especially since I won't…"

Kurt sat up on the couch and pushed her onto the coffee table and screamed, "I want to kill you" as he shook with anger. He walked into the bedroom, got dressed and left the house with some of his things.

Kurt used the fight as an excuse to leave but Alexis knew it was because he was uncomfortable with her knowing the truth about him. As long as Alexis portrayed Kurt as a great guy her value was high. NPD's value people according to how much affirmation they receive from them, it is called supply. When they are not receiving any sort of supply from people, they devalue those people like throw away paper plates once used and actually begin to hate them because they have no use for them if they cannot get some sort of supply from them. It is a fact that people are made up of both good and bad, however, NPD's cannot believe this; it means death to them. It is impossible for them to believe that there will be times when people get on your nerves or disagree with you as in normal everyday life. To them, people are either valued or de-valued; and the way they determine that is by how often people agree with them, affirm them, like them, think the way they do, etc. If someone disagrees with them or rebukes them for some reason, that person all of a sudden becomes someone they don't like anymore. So whenever Alexis communicated any negative thoughts, or complained about anything toward Kurt, he automatically devalued her and his supposed love was turned off like a switch. A few days later, Kurt brought divorce papers over for her to sign which she did not sign because she did not trust him.

She knew enough about psychology to know that when someone says they want to kill you, you should take them seriously. Alexis knew in her heart that a line had been crossed. A line she could never step back over, however she was not at the place where her heart wanted to allow what her head was telling her. She called her friend Calahan. He suggested she meet with the elders at church; an appointment was scheduled.

About this time, a friend of Alexis' who was an attorney knew she was unemployed and asked her to do some research. The job entailed a lot of copying of criminal records and dealing with criminal charges. It took her two and a half months to complete but part of what she had to do was type cases into a computer system which included what action a person did to warrant a charge being brought against them. She realized that God had brought her to this job so she could see the seriousness of Kurt's behavior. She could have had him arrested many times and charges filed against him. Invoking fear of bodily injury through verbal means was a felony.

During the meeting with the elders, they advised her not to sign the divorce papers unless she had an attorney look at them first. She played back for them the angry and threatening phone messages Kurt had left. It was kind of hard for them to believe because Kurt was so different in front of everyone else than he was with Alexis at home. They referred her to a doctor who had more credentials than his office walls would hold and a doctorate in diagnosing psychosis knowing that this situation was above their heads psychologically and beyond the scope of what they could help her with. Unlike the last counselor, this guy was scary in that he exuded intelligence that made you know he could sum you up in a very short period of time.

There was a packet of information that they both had to fill out. Alexis completed her forms and submitted them with this letter:

"Dear Dr. Billings:

I am coming to you in hopes of making some sense out of my present situation. My husband and I are separated and have been for about a month. This is one of many times. I do not trust Kurt and I believe he is mentally unstable. I'm not talking about the weaknesses we all struggle with from time to time, I'm talking about mental instability. I have to make a decision about whether or not I am going to remain married. I don't know if it is even safe or healthy to work on this marriage any longer. Some of the behavior that causes me to wonder if he is safe to be around is, he has pushed me several times, once so hard that I fell on the ground. He has thrown his wedding ring in the toilet, smashed it flat with a hammer and recently told me he wanted to kill me. These are just the most recent things that come to mind. He does not think that he is accountable for the things he does when he is in a rage attack because he is mad, and he says he is mad because it is my fault."

CHAPTER SIX

Today I officially stopped loving you
Our supposed love depreciated before my eyes
As I heard you speak that last angry word
This time I didn't even cry

Your apologies mean nothing
They fly like the wind
Up and down the caverns in my heart
Created by the impurities I've allowed in

I ask God to make robes from my rags
I beg Him to begin
To heal the pain that you caused
The day after I let you walk in

The things that are important to me
You just don't take part
Any need I have, even if simple
Is a strain to your heart

How I wish I could go back
And erase the past four years
With its heartache, pain and sorrow
Back to a world without fears

Fear of wasting my time with
Your love that is not pure
Fear that I can never get back
What's been lost or destroyed, can I endure?

To get back to where love was abundant
Patience, kindness and truth running solid
You've tried to be what you can't
How was I to know you were invalid

The attitude of hate
You seem to hold onto

Discredits all of your claims
The lack of spiritual fruit provides the clue

Our most recent nonsensical fight
Was the last straw I guess
The camel's back is broken
I surrender to God and finally confess.

Dr. Billings agreed to meet on a Thursday evening after work.

"So, tell me about your situation."

"Like I said in my letter, I don't know what to do at this point. I don't know if I should even stay married to this person; I am afraid. I have two kids to think about. I know God says He hates divorce, so I want to do everything I can to make this work and I don't want to do anything that will jeopardize my relationship with God."

In a way, that was a joke; Alexis had already done enough to jeopardize her relationship with God by participating in viewing pornography, arguing, etc. She went on in detail to explain some of the problems in the relationship as Dr. Billings stared at her with great interest. As far as he knew, it was distinctly possible that she was the one who was crazy and detached from reality.

And so there were many appointments with Dr. Billings and Alexis discovered a lot about herself including why Kurt was attracted to her in the first place. During these months of counseling, and only after the onset of the appointments with Dr. Billings, Alexis began having explicit spiritual dreams. "I know there are those who say that God does not communicate with us except through His word, and would never speak to us in a dream, however, I know without a doubt that these dreams were spiritual and that God allowed me to remember them. They are different from my dreams that do not make sense, or a dream in the middle of the night that isn't remembered. These dreams seemed specific, always right before I fully woke up, clear and precise."

Dr. Billings was not shocked by this, in fact, it was almost as if he fully expected it and was prepared to discuss them as he retrieved many books on the subject. "The dreams come at different times and seem to guide me." Alexis told him. She wrote the dreams down as best she could remember in a dream log and discussed them with Dr. Billings with each occurrence.

Journal Entry - Dream:

I was walking on a mountainous road and saw two animals kind of like badgers but they were grayish, like they had absolutely no life in them, however, you could see their dangerous looking teeth and they were very much alive and fighting together and coming toward me as if they were purposely going to attack me but they were busy with one another. I thought to myself I'd better step up off of the ground and get to higher ground away from them. I did not have the thought they were personally after me but more like they were coming in my direction and I was just in their path. Once I made that first and second step upward I was all of a sudden up on top of a higher place than where I had stepped originally. Then all of a sudden I went even higher soaring upward, higher, higher still. I got as far up as a major jet airplane and was flying along side the plane. I was close to one of the windows and could see a Middle Eastern type looking guy on the other side of the window; I knew he represented my enemy; this was shortly after the 9-11 attack. I could not tell if he could see me or not but it appeared that he could not. I wasn't afraid to stare intently at him and I was singing a song the youth group sings in their Sunday morning class about God, "You are Holy", echo, "You are worthy", echo, "Worthy of praise", "I will trust you", echo, "I will love you", echo, "all of my days"... angels were singing the echo part and then the dream ended.

"Dr. Billings, I know that in my life anytime I have been in a situation where I needed help from God it seemed like God wanted me to take the first step and then He took over from there. In this dream, I barely stepped upward and was whisked away upward immediately in a powerful way. This dream cemented my thoughts of getting away from Kurt. He does not have power or control over me anymore."

Journal Entry - Dream: This dream occurred the night I took on the job with the attorney.

There were huge swimming pools of water that had been prepared for swimming. No one had been swimming in them yet. I was there with someone. The pools were huge shell shapes and all attached to one another. You could tell they were sparkling clean and there were five of them. The one closest to us was not ready for

138

swimming yet because it had not been cleaned. The maintenance guy, who had a comforting peaceful smile, who I took to represent Jesus, said it would not take long and that we could swim in one of the other pools while we were waiting, that it would be ready soon. We would have to go to one of the other pools for now. The person I was with made mention that she could not afford the payment of the cost to swim and I had prepared myself to pay her way. She became disabled at that point and I had to carry her but the person I was carrying became me. I carried her toward one of the cleaned pools that we could swim in. I had not told her yet that I was going to pay her way.

Alexis explained to Dr. Billings, "There are five areas that I pray for: spiritually, financially, emotionally, mentally and physically. I took this dream to mean that the five pools represented these areas for me and it was the financial pool that had not been cleaned yet. I think this dream is telling me that even though I want to end things right now, that God still has some things He wants to show me through the new job and the relationship. The message I received from this dream, however, unnerving as it is, is to wait a little while, that it is not yet time."

Journal Entry - Dream:

"I pulled a piece of bread out of a loaf that I had previously eaten from. It was two-thirds full. The piece of bread had little bites out of it but not all the way through the bread to the other side. I held it up and looked at it thinking to myself that it looked like

139

something had been eating at it. I showed it to someone else who confirmed what I already knew and we then examined the loaf of bread. At quick glance, it looked like a normal loaf of bread but in the corner of the bag, hiding in the bread was an ugly dark colored mouse burrowed in a ball trying to use the bread to hide in. It was not moving. Discussion took place that whether the mouse was dead or alive the loaf of bread had to be thrown out because it was ruined either way. If dead, it would rot in there, if alive, you could not eat bread that a mouse had been living in. I felt disgust at the thought that I had eaten out of it previously.

When I awoke, the first thought I had was to take the loaf of bread to the fire pit out back and burn it. The rodent represented Kurt and the bread represented life. He is slowly eating away at my life with his pernicious ways. Sometimes I feel helpless to do anything about this. This dream scared me because of its obvious conclusion. If the bread represented my life, according to the dream, my life was ruined either way because of Kurt. If the bread represented his life, there was no hope he would ever overcome this disorder."

At the explanation of this dream, Alexis was shook up and began crying in Dr. Billings' office and after the appointment that afternoon Dr. Billings scheduled a follow up appointment for the next day in addition to the regular appointments, just to make sure Alexis was ok.

Journal Entry - Follow up dream to above: "This dream occurred last night I believe as an immediate follow up to the loaf of bread dream. I guess I somewhat panicked in thinking that my life was ruined either way and I was without hope. Thanks be to God that we can be forgiven because of the blood of Christ and restored back to a right relationship with Him.

I was looking up at a house similar to where we use to live in Montana called Saddle Mountain whereby you could see the houses on the side of the mountain from the main road below. I could see smoke coming up from the house and had the feeling that the house was ruined or going to burn. It was my house. Suddenly a woman, short dark hair and glasses, not masculine or feminine looking, picked up the house, put it down on the ground in front of me and put the fire out. She was obviously not limited by size if she could pick up a house like a giant. The house was not ruined. Once she placed the house on the ground in front of me, it became the size of a two-story bird feeder made of wood, not fancy but not run down. I remember feeling glad to know it was not ruined, but feeling odd that my house was the size of a bird feeder."

Alexis continued her thoughts out loud to Dr. Billings, "I believe the person in this dream represented an angel and this was God's way of showing me His angels are watching over me and that He will take care of any problems and that his grace is sufficient to cover my sins no matter how big they seem to me. I believe this dream was prompted by Kurt saying he was taking half of the house. I believe God was letting me know that all would be well and that the threats of Kurt are smaller than he tries to make them out to be."

"I don't want to startle you Alexis, just keep in mind that if Kurt can prove that he has contributed to at least half of the mortgage payments, he absolutely can try to take half of the house."

That night Alexis prayed diligently: "Dear Lord, I am overwhelmed and in awe of your goodness, mercy and grace. Please help me to move forward toward you in spite of Kurt's threats and intimidation. Please help me to have a way to financially support my family and protect that which you have already blessed me with. Please continue to clean that last pool and get it ready for swimming. Thank you for all you have done, in Jesus' name, Amen."

Dear God, father I love you and am in awe of your forgiveness and discipline and love. I pray you will bless me in a way that I will be able to take care of the children you have blessed me with and live a life pleasing in your sight. Thank you, in Jesus' name, Amen.

It came time to see if Kurt would come for a visit with Dr. Billings. By this time, Kurt had started to want to talk to Alexis and work things out; she wasn't sure, but he agreed to see Dr. Billings and had changed his mind about divorcing Alexis. Part of her wanted him to come just so she could get an answer about what she suspected: that Kurt was mentally unstable; another part wanted vindication that she was not the crazy one as Kurt had tried to portray.

During the visit with Kurt, Dr. Billings asked them to discuss what they thought was wrong with the relationship. One of the many issues Alexis presented was the fact that she had asked him not to throw lint on the floor out of his pockets which she found all over the house, but instead of respecting her request, Kurt did it more after she asked him not to. To Alexis, the big deal was not the lint on the floor, but the sadistic behavior responsible for Kurt doing something on purpose that she had asked him not to do and the obvious insensitivity to her needs. Kurt would also weed eat her flowers down the the ground and laugh about it out loud.

This was just one of the many examples of sadistic thinking that permeated who Kurt was. Alexis went on to ask Kurt in front of Dr. Billings why he acted this way. It seemed to her like he wanted to ruin anything that made her happy, and that being sadistic made him happy. Being put on the spot like this in front of someone other than his family, who were as sadistic as he was, made him uncomfortable and mad, and he raged with anger at the thought that Alexis had been right about him and the apparent conclusion of his diagnosis, to the point where he had to get up and leave the office. When he came back in, he asked, "So, what are we saying, that I'm crazy?"

After a few appointments together, Dr. Billings requested to see Alexis alone. Kurt laughed at this and said, "See, you are the crazy one. He wants to see you alone."

Dr. Billings wanted to see Alexis alone primarily to tell her to run! And run fast as the last counselor had told her, but he never came right out and said it in those words. "Dr. Billings, I know that Kurt's behavior is abusive and sadistic, there's no doubt about that, I noticed that in the beginning of the marriage, however, I am

143

confused about why I even got with him to begin with. And now that I am with him, why do I stay with him knowing that he is abusive. Is it strictly because God says He hates divorce? Why am I with this person?" Alexis was holding her arms out in question.

Through Dr. Billings' counseling, Alexis discovered a strong hold that had imprisoned her all these years from her childhood: one specific event she witnessed as an eight-year-old child. "We lived in Vermont at the time and I loved it. The mountains with their warm fire colors in fall, white birch trees in summer, tree limbs heavy from the snow in winter, Clydesdale horses so majestic and snorty, and maple trees. This was where my mother taught me to crochet, where I learned how to balance on a thin flat piece of wood as it flowed down the brook at the base of the mountain; where I taught my dog Brandy how to ride a tricycle; collected one hundred salamanders in a little red wagon; and constructed roads in the dirt for matchbox cars and trucks. This is where I wandered for hours by myself in the mountains admiring God's creation or visiting the hippies down the street who were very nice to me and very freedom oriented."

With her eyes closed, she explained further, "I did not understand why my mother seemed unhappy all the time; why she cried a lot. She had started living with a man who I was to call Uncle which was weird to me because he was not my uncle. There was loud arguing and I was in my room. As I came out to the front of the trailer we were living in, I saw him open the door; I can see the snow outside. He picked my mother up by the hair of the head and her crouch and threw her out of the door into the snow headfirst. I

144

watched in disbelief and horror as she cried; I could do nothing. He was standing between my mother and me. My mother was crying as she stood back up. I don't remember what she was saying or the details about what happened after that. Why did she stay with him after that?" Alexis began sobbing; she had no idea that this one scene was hidden deep inside of her for all these years and played such a vital role in her adult life.

"You are not that little girl anymore Alexis. That little girl was powerless to do anything about that situation. You are not powerless anymore." Dr. Billings spoke scripture over her and prayed that God would release her from this stronghold from childhood.

Over the course of the rest of her counseling, Alexis watched domestic abuse videos and discovered a lot about her mother, who as it turned out had the same personality disorder that Kurt was diagnosed with, just to a lesser degree. She became aware of how those dynamics were fleshed out in her life and in her relationships especially with men. Dr. Billings also educated her on Post Traumatic Stress Syndrome (PTSS). If a person has lived with another person who has NPD, they are more than likely experiencing a certain amount of PTSS.

Journal Entry – Dream:

"In the driveway of the house, I was sending Kurt away. He tripped as he walked toward his truck and fell hard smashing his groin area into the concrete as if someone had dropped a boulder on

145

top of him in only that area. He was severely injured and laying on the ground. For a moment, I thought he was dying but he got up and was standing by the truck leaned over on it trying to recover, which he did. The kids were looking at me as if to say, mom he is hurt, aren't you going to do something. I shook my head left to right and without sympathy walked into the house."

Journal Entry:

I learned the truth about Kurt in February. It was April when I spilled my guts about it to him. From April through September we would be separated more than together with a couple different short periods of attempted reconciliation that only lasted three to four weeks. Kurt, was, in fact professionally diagnosed as psychotic and unsafe to be around. During the last three weeks we were together my daughter was in a horse show and we were on our way there. Dr. Billings was not very happy that I had allowed Kurt back in the house; I was even unsure about why I had done it but post traumatic stress syndrome can do strange things to a person's thinking patterns and until a person gets to that place where they are done, they are not done. My daughter had gone up to the equestrian center earlier that morning. As previously stated, Kurt seemed to want to ruin anything good in my life and this included my relationship with my children, so he started a fight over something stupid by the time we arrived at the first stop sign by our house. He then turned the vehicle off in the middle of the road, took the keys and started walking home leaving me sitting in the vehicle. I knew him well enough by now to know that his goal was to make me late for my daughter's horse show which in turn would negatively affect my relationship with my daughter. He envied that relationship therefore he hated that relationship and subconsciously needed to try to ruin it; although it was no use to talk to him about it because he would never admit the behavior. I sat there for a second in shock, but then something finally clicked and I had had enough just the way Dr. Billings knew it would happen. Kurt was purposely trying to make me late to prevent me from seeing my daughter in the horse show and was doing whatever he had to do to get that to happen.

I got out of the vehicle, started walking to the house to get my extra set of keys. He went back to the vehicle and drove around the block. I was close to the house when he drove by slowly, laughing.

I looked him directly in the eye and stated, "I am divorcing you." This event was the straw that broke the camel's back. This was the scene that caused me to get to the place I needed to be, to finally be done.

This made him change his continence. "Don't divorce me, please don't divorce me." It wasn't that he didn't want me to divorce him because he loved me, he didn't want me to divorce him because then he would have to find someone else with which to supply him with what he needed to survive. "Ok, if you do, I have already talked with an attorney and I'm taking half the house."

That scene ended with him going to the horse show with me and behaving like a scolded child that wanted to get out of trouble,

147

bending over backwards to make me happy. He even bought my daughter an expensive riding helmet while at the show. You might think I am crazy to have even allowed him to go with me, however, I did what I needed to do to get to my daughter's horse show on time, which I did, but knew at this point I was done with this relationship and would be proceeding with a divorce. It was a relief as much as it was possible to find relief in realizing that you had gone very astray from where you needed to be and had just spent the last four and a half years of your life with a psychotic person who you exposed your children to.

I was confused because originally I had thought I could make this marriage work and wanted to please God by not going through another divorce, but slowly it became apparent to me that if I stayed with Kurt, I would be going against God, and the original sin was getting with him in the first place. How did staying with him make it any better? If you find you are going in the wrong direction, how does continuing down that road make the situation any better? Kurt was not who he purported to be; he didn't love God or live for God. He was a deceiver and had no intentions of living for God. For me to stay with him after learning of the truth was sin. The marriage should have been annulled five months after it started.

I met with one of the elders of the church and let him know that I planned on filing for divorce. One of the things that Dr. Billings dealt with was people in the church telling woman that they must stay married to men, even if they are abusive, because God states he hates divorce. I wanted the elders to know exactly why I was divorcing Kurt. I never received the elder's blessing. They said they would never condone the divorce but understood why I was doing it. That in itself was good enough for me. I actually had one of the elders meet with Dr. Billings though, so that he understood I was not selling out of a difficult marriage situation, but reacting to a physically unsafe and emotionally unhealthy environment.

As soon as I could after the horse show event when Kurt said he was going to take half the house, the house that as a single mom I had worked so hard for, long before Kurt came along, I filed for divorce. While he was packing up some of his things he said, "It doesn't have to be this way. You don't have to divorce me." Then he asked me if I wanted to have sex. I unemotionally said no.

My neighbor who knew the situation and who had seen Kurt's truck parked in the street came over from her house. "Is everything ok?" She asked me.

"Yes, I'm fine. I'm finally doing it; I've had enough." I said when Kurt went back to his vehicle. "You are a notary right?"

"Yeah."

"Ok. Will you notarize these papers Kurt needs to sign?"

She went back to her house to get her stamp and Kurt signed the papers. I took the papers to the courthouse as fast as I could and filed them.

Waiting thirty days after that was a nightmare as he continually called me leaving messages even though I asked him not to. I finally wrote a note, kept a copy and sent it through the mail stating that he was not to contact me in anyway, shape or form. I met

149

with one of the elders and let them know that I would press charges against him if he did not stop harassing me.

Journal Entry - Dream: After distressing days just days after the divorce was final.

A man fully clothed in a white robe, his hands the only thing uncovered, you could not see the head, only from the chest area down to his hands, his arms bent at the elbows, sitting at a table. The man was holding his hands out giving something, not offering but giving. On the counter in front of the hands was a perfect yellow rose, stem bluntly cut at the right height if you wanted to put it in a vase, the bloom was perfect, not fully opened yet but ready to open soon. God was giving me His peace.

Journal Entry - Dream: This dream came two months after the divorce was final.

I was flying around the perimeter of a large green beautiful pasture, along the white well kept, if not new, fence. I was not in a body while I was flying and it was as if someone was showing me this place like it was already mine or going to be mine. There was a road built along the property. You could tell the pasture area and house was older than the new road. The new road was a strip and not necessarily for cars, maybe horses. It had a fence on both sides and new mulch evenly spread over it. Each fence was different like on the outside perimeter it was tall and light colored wood, the inside I believe was chain linked. This new road was well protected. If you were in the pasture you could clearly see if someone was on the road but if you had been on the other side of the tall fence you would not have been able to tell necessarily if someone was on the road unless on horseback perhaps. Off in the distance, nestled in the trees outside of the white fence in the direction the road led was a house. It appeared to be a Cape Cod type house but you really could not tell much about it except for the fact that it all seemed very peaceful. The grass was very green like the color of brand new grass but it was tall.

Journal Entry:

This dream was difficult to figure out because of its complexity. Part of the success of narcissistic personality disorder is that they wound their victim's self esteem and confidence to the point where you regress emotionally and mentally and second guess yourself and while I knew I made the right decision, I started spiraling downward after that, wondering if I knew anything at all, let alone what was from God and what was not from God. With the guilt that I felt over the sin I committed in this relationship, I did not feel worthy of any of God's blessings; not even worthy enough for God to let me live; I deserved death and I knew that. I felt separated from God. I also was recovering from post traumatic stress syndrome from living with a psychotic person for four and a half years. It took me a long time to embrace the grace and mercy that was extended to me by God because of Christ dying on the cross and to get it in my head that I could never be good enough to earn God's love even if this relationship had not taken place. It would be two years after the divorce when I finally got this through my heart. You can intellectualize it in your head all day long but to really feel it in your heart is another matter entirely. This dream represented newness, protection and peace but it would take time. When Samson turned from God and his hair was cut, his hair eventually grew back; however, the hair only grew so many inches at a time.

The time following Alexis' divorce was dry as a desert. To her, it seemed God had left her. If she could feel this forsaken by the sin of divorce, and the sins committed within the marriage, it was inconceivable to her how Christ must have felt taking on the sins of the whole world. The divorce was final on November fourteenth. Two days after the divorce, Alexis had the following short but sweet dream:

Journal Entry - Dream:
I looked in the back yard after hearing movement in the night and saw a fox and a deer peacefully sleeping in the yard together. It was a comforting dream.

For Thanksgiving that year the kids would be traveling out of state with their father, which would make Alexis feel even that much more alone. She spent a couple days out of town visiting her father, which helped a little. He was very reasonable to talk to. "It is going to take time to heal and there is nothing you can do to speed that process; just do the best you can." He would say.

It wasn't like Alexis doubted whether or not she had done the right thing. She knew she made the right decision in divorcing Kurt, if for no other reason, for the safety of her children. But it made her feel so cold to realize the genesis of the sin. She could have avoided the sin of divorce by avoiding the relationship in the beginning where she was led astray by her own lusts and desires (some people call it falling in love), ignoring the pig face image. Alexis did not deny that the phenomenon of falling in love happened, she just viewed it differently now. Every "falling in love" experience starts the same way. You long to see the person, there is a dancing of sorts that goes on between the two parties. There is nothing significant about it, it does not hold a relationship together and it is not an indication that the relationship will be good for either party or that that person would be an asset in someone's life. Consistency over time is still the best revealer. Falling in love is a natural occurrence that happens everyday, and can happen with more than one person for most people.

Even if the experience is approached in a practical way, as Alexis had done, the outcome is only in your control so much as it depends on you. One person does not have control over another, so there is risk involved; a risk that Alexis planned never to take again. She struggled to make sense out of the whole falling in love and desiring another person scene. If James says that we are led astray by our own lusts and desires, then in a sense, isn't "falling in love" considered the desiring of another person and a bad thing?

Alexis started a new job three months after the divorce was final. The assortment of suits she had acquired over the years served to produce a professional appearance. She enjoyed this new job and for the first time in a long time looked forward to going to work everyday. The management treated their employees like adults and that was refreshing. No more having to announce to everyone that you had to use the restroom, having assigned lunch times and someone looking over your shoulder all the time. It was almost like having your own business within a business.

During a lunch room conversation one day approximately three weeks after she started the job, the conversation turned to music. "Isn't there anyone here who likes country music?" Alexis asked jokingly, seeing as how everyone's opinion seemed to be negative toward it. A quiet gentleman named Morrison raised his hand as if he was in a classroom and the teacher was asking a question. "I do." He responded.

With that response a conversation ensued between him and Alexis that would produce many offspring conversations like fertility drugs had been given for such and been successful.

When Alexis first gazed into Morrison's eyes that first time, it was equivalent to a warm glowing fireplace; she found solace there for whatever reason and peace came over her. As they talked, she noticed his eyes appeared to have an absence of anger, an absence of the look a man has when he is addicted to pornography; a look she was all too familiar with. The scripture, "The eyes are a light unto the soul", came to her mind.

Alexis wasn't sure what was going on but as days passed she felt as if she were falling in love with Morrison. She did not tell him or anyone else for that matter and tried hard not to let it show realizing in a sense she was very vulnerable right now only three months after her divorce. In addition, Morrison was not her type at all. He smoked, drove a motorcycle, which she hated, had numerous tattoos, which she hated more than motorcycles, and cussed. Why in the world would she be the slightest bit attracted to him she wondered; she couldn't figure it out and was suspicious. She had to admit that the thought of demonic activity crossed her mind. She was deceived once, what prevented her from being deceived again? Was this one of Satan's schemes?

Alexis considered what she had learned about Post Traumatic Stress Syndrome and realized that the confusion she was experiencing was part of that syndrome. However, it was refreshing that a man knew she did not drink, smoke or cuss and yet did not change his behavior just to be in accordance to hers or to what he thought she would like. That is what Kurt had done to purposely deceive her and make her think he was what he wasn't. There was also a searching for truth within Morrison during their spiritual conversations; maybe this in itself was the reason she was attracted to him. Whatever the reason, there was definitely a connection in Morrison's eyes.

Over the next few weeks there would be flirting at work, several phone conversations after work, a soft touch on the shoulder as one of them walked by the other, and eye contact that signified there was an attraction, although Alexis was not physically attracted to Morrison at all.

Alexis continued seeing Dr. Billings for awhile after her divorce and had told him about Morrison from the start. Dr. Billings thought it was much too soon for her to be interested in anyone.

"How are you?" Dr. Billings asked at Alexis' next appointment.

"Doing ok except I have a lot of questions as usual." Alexis plopped down into the chair, slipped her shoes off and curled her legs up under her.

"What are your questions?"

"What if Morrison is one of Satan's workers?"

"Are there any specific words or actions that would make you believe this?" Dr. Billings asked.

"Kind of. But it is hard to determine whether or not the spiritual energy flow whether positive or negative is from God or just everyday life."

"I would not waste too much time on trying to determine by vague uncertainties whether or not someone is a worker of Satan or God's child. The word of the Lord is true and the truth is always revealed in time by the fruit produced by the individual."

Alexis did not want to devote time to Morrison if in fact he was a worker of Satan. "I suppose you are right. But it seems strange

156

doesn't it the connection to the eyes as if he was casting a spell on me."

"God does not want us to walk around in confusion and God is not the God of confusion. Satan is the father of lies which he has been from the beginning, and it's those lies that cause confusion."

Alexis reflected on what Dr. Billings said, and then thought of something. "You know, there are a couple of things about him that might suggest a problem."

"Like what?"

"Well...I call my daughter baby girl and after he heard me call her this on the phone one time, he called me by that name, which was very weird because I never heard him use those words before that time."

"We have discussed this before, but you are very well aware that you will continue to attract the same type of man that you have attracted over and over and you cannot stop their attraction to you, you can only learn to recognize them on the surface before you get too involved with someone."

"Yes, you have told me this. I will be careful and pray about it."

In her research one of the many things Alexis had learned, was that one of the reasons men with Narcissistic Personality Disorder were attracted to her was because she was a strong person in her identity. She knew her likes, her dislikes, and for the most part did not feel imprisoned by what other people thought about her; people with NPD feel imprisoned by the opinions of others and have to be liked by others. She had strong opinions about matters and stuck to them. Also, she did not have to be popular or liked, to be happy. NPD's have severe identity crisis and are attracted to people with strong identities. They then try to take on that strong person's identity by wanting to be them and imitating them, however, once envy is conceived it always gives birth to hate, so NPD's wind up hating the very thing they felt they needed to attach themselves to for an identity to survive. It is a vicious cycle and an impossible existence.

The rest of the session with Dr. Billings was spent discussing post traumatic stress syndrome and how it manifests itself in the everyday lives of those experiencing it. It was impossible for Dr. Billings to tell Alexis how long it would take her to process the syndrome, but it was very possible that her attraction to Morrison could have been nothing more than her mind's way of trying to heal.

Approximately three weeks after Alexis noticed the look in Morrison's eyes, they were leaving the office at the same time. He walked close to her as they walked out the door of the building which was in the back. When she turned to say good-bye, he put his hand on her waist and gently pressed his lips against hers. She was shocked, did not kiss him back, and just walked away to her car not saying anything. He ran after her apologizing. "I'm so sorry. Everyone makes mistakes." He was falling all over himself.

Alexis prayed and analyzed the situation on the drive home. "Dear Father in Heaven, I must be losing my mind. Is this another of Satan's tricks, another way to deceive me? God please do not allow me to be deceived again and don't let me deceive myself by being led away by my own lusts and desires. I want to do the right thing but I'm not sure what's going on here." It was the type of prayer she should have prayed with Kurt but was too ignorant to know.

Once over the shock of it, the spontaneous kiss made her smile and she admitted she was attracted to the boldness of it, but then another thought popped into her mind. What if, this was in fact the same type of man she attracts and Morrison was actually jealous that she interviewed a gorgeous actor today, who had just left the office before they did. That's crazy she told herself, however, this would be indicative behavior of an NPD. It drove her insane that she could not see through people to their hearts, to the truth of everything like God could. She was incompetent to decipher and judge thoughts and intentions of other people's hearts and so time would be the only way she would know what type of fruit would be generated by this person.

Morrison asked Alexis to go with him for coffee after work two weeks later. She accepted and he kissed her as soon as he saw her right there in the parking lot of the restaurant. This made Alexis uncomfortable because she wasn't much for public displays of affection but she did not stop him this time and actually kissed him back. However, there was something that just did not ever feel right about the whole thing.

After seeing Morrison for approximately three dates, there were a few more signs that Alexis recognized. She prayed continually about it and came to the conclusion that Morrison was a test. He was in fact that same type of man she always attracts, however, she just did not know to what degree because there are different levels of the disorder. There was the accidental hit on the arm where she said, "Ouch that hurt." And he said, "No it didn't", instead of, "Oh sorry, I didn't mean to hurt you." Invalidation of other people's feelings was a sign. NPD's only allow themselves to feel, not others. If they acknowledge other peoples feelings, that means they are attached. Since they possess no true identity it is impossible for another person to ever make a true connection with them or for them to ever be truly emotionally attached.

There was also Alexis' request not to kiss her at work or in front of their co-workers. He did not honor that request and respect her boundaries. NPD's do not respect other people's boundaries and are in fact jealous of them because they do not know how to install their own boundaries. This was another sign and made Alexis think back to Kurt and a time before they started dating when they went as friends to a civil war re-enactment. While they were sitting on the ground, some three year old kid, that Kurt did not even know started jumping all over him. It was cute for the first five seconds however, the kid continued the behavior for almost an hour. Alexis wondered why Kurt did not tell the kid to stop. The parents, who were sitting right there, weren't doing anything about it either. Alexis remembered how bothered she was by this, but did not know why she was bothered until after her research about NPD. Kurt was incapable of erecting a boundary against the child's behavior even though he did not want the child to continue the behavior toward him. Kurt was not allowed as a child to erect any limitations on the way other's treated him or stop someone from mistreating him.

Alexis knew that it was way too soon to get involved with anyone else just months after her divorce, so she used this as the excuse to end the dating relationship with Morrison. While this was in fact true, it was not the primary reason she quit seeing him. He did not take the news very well and it made working together very awkward for a long time. Morrison tried to skew the reality that Alexis did not want to be anything more than friends but Alexis was insistent and eventually he accepted that message.

LESSONS FROM THE LAWN – CONCLUSION

It took Alexis two years to get the lawn back to where it needed to be just like it took her two years to feel healed from the relationship with Kurt once it was finally over. However, Alexis never got the lawn to a state of perfection like it was when the house was first built; it was a constant maintenance issue falling prey to certain outside components like lack of rain, too much rain, weeds and bugs. Just when she would take care of one weed, another type would pop up. Or if she waited too long to put down pesticide, the bugs started to kill the grass. Then if she did spread the chemicals and there was a lot of rain, it washed everything away and the weeds went wild. In the summer, it was too hot to even bother with it and the abundance of rain from the tropical storms created a mess with everyone's yard not just hers. Too much water was almost worse than not enough. She wondered if maintaining the yard was worth it, just to have a nice looking lawn she could walk on barefoot.

Paralleling her lawn and her life, in conclusion, Alexis' spiritual understanding was that as long as we are here on this earth in these bodies, we are going to have trials and tests constantly; there's no way around it and we will be tempted to grow weary just like she was growing weary with the upkeep of her lawn. Likewise, our spiritual lawn will continue to be bombarded by Satan's attempts to kill, steal and destroy anything good in our lives. Nothing was going to be perfect until Heaven. Alexis' lawn was going to need constant maintenance on a regular schedule just like Alexis needed

162

constant spiritual maintenance in reading God's word, prayer and fellowship with like minded people on a regular basis.

"Let us not grow weary while doing good, for in due season we shall reap if we do not lose heart." Galatians 6:9

It was not comforting to Alexis to know that combating weeds in her lawn was going to be a life long process or for as long as she owned the house, however, it was comforting to her to know that no-one can pluck her from God's hand.

Romans 8.38: For I am convinced that neither death, nor life, nor angels, nor principalities, nor powers, nor things present, nor things to come, nor height, nor depth, nor any other created thing shall be able to separate us from the love of God which is in Christ Jesus our Lord.

Satan had tried to get Alexis to believe that there was not enough grace to cover her relationship with Kurt…that she had gone too far into sin, that she was now marred never to be clean again as in the dream about the mouse spoiling the loaf of bread. But it is by His wounds that we are healed, by His death and bloodshed that our sins are forgiven, by His burial that our sins are thrown to the depths of the sea as far as the east is from the west, and it is by His resurrection that we are justified, raised again to walk in newness of life so that when God looks at us He sees His son and not our sin. Alexis' righteousness or attempt to be good had nothing to do with it; it is the righteousness of Christ that makes us clean and worthy.

CHAPTER SEVEN

The coffee smelled especially sweet that day as Alexis, who had not slept well the night before walked into the bagel shop. It was over two years after the divorce and the post traumatic stress syndrome was healed. She had not been interested in anyone since the brief couple of weeks with Morrison two years ago and was just now coming to a place where she even began noticing guys. The friends she typically sat with all said hello as she walked over to the counter to order her bagel and coffee noticing an attractive man sitting at the counter she had not seen before.

"The usual Alexis?" Asked the clerk as Alexis turned from looking at the man.

"Yes please." Alexis handed the money to her, put the change in her purse, then sat at the table where her friends were sitting, and listened as she ate. There was a serious discussion going on regarding something from the local newspaper.

"They're all sick I tell ya." Claimed Joe.

"Just think about all the ones that don't get caught." Added Leroy.

"I don't understand how a fifty-two year old man could get turned on by a seven year old." Betty said.

After several minutes of listening to the conversation and then reading the newspaper article they were all talking about, Alexis could hold back no longer. "Do you know that one hundred percent of the time the people arrested for sexual crimes are addicted to pornography?"

Leroy was the first to respond to her. "What? You're crazy!" He laughed as he moved his hand in the air toward her like he was pushing her away.

"It's true; have you ever researched it?" Alexis offered.

Betty, who worked for the local newspaper, was intrigued. "What do you base that statement on?"

"Let's just call it, years of research."

Alexis was unaware that the man at the counter she had noticed earlier was listening to the conversation as the debate about the matter grew louder with Alexis defending her belief that a huge percentage of men are addicted to pornography. She believed that the increase in pornography addiction was the reason why sexual crime statistics were also on the increase.

"As a matter of fact, I'll go one step further and tell you that those men who are arrested for sexual crimes all have the same look about their eyes and therefore men who are addicted to pornography all have the same look. I can pick it out of a crowd." Now they were really making fun of her and saying she was crazy.

"Do I have the look?" Joe asked mockingly as he posed and flashed his eyes. Everyone laughed.

Alexis, who was now the table's laughing stock, dropped the subject and let the conversation move on to something else; they really did not understand. She knew that unless someone experienced living with an individual who was addicted to pornography, or researched the subject themselves, they would never understand.

Everyone but Alexis eventually dispersed from the table to start their day. She sat there for awhile finishing the portion of the paper she hadn't read. When it came time for her to go, she began gathering her belongings but then felt a tap on her shoulder.

"Cuse me ma'am." A man said.

Alexis turned around and saw the attractive man she noticed when she first came in standing there; she had forgotten about him. He looked familiar up close and had a clean cut refreshing look; the accent was Texan for sure but refined a little for some reason like he had been trained in speaking at one time or another. He wore a pair of Wrangler jeans, a crisp short sleeved blue and white stripped button down shirt untucked with the top few buttons undone, short sleeved navy blue t-shirt slightly showing underneath. His black cowboy boots had a small shinny silver symbol on them that Alexis couldn't quite make out without staring. His skin tone was either tan or naturally darker than most, and he smelled fantastic. His hair was dark and very short, almost as if it had been cut in a crew cut not long before. She had a hard time guessing his approximate age because in a way he looked thirty-ish and in a way he looked fifty-ish; either way she noticed he was definitely in good shape.

"Hi. Yer gonna think I'm weird or something but I overheard yer conversation a little while ago and I'm curious about what ya said about men havin a look if they're addicted to pornography."

166

"Why?" She asked hesitantly and in a protective way studying his face. He had obviously been eavesdropping and she felt violated and uncomfortable; briefly forgetting about the fact that he was extremely attractive.

He didn't answer but instead threw another question at her. "Do ya have a minute or ya gettin ready to leave?"

"I am actually off work today; I was just leaving because everyone else had gone, but I don't know you; you're a complete stranger to me, and it's kind of weird that you were eavesdropping on the conversation." Alexis wondered if he was some kind of freak or something but at the same time thought it would be a complete waste if someone that good looking turned out to be a freak, so she wanted to give him a chance.

"It's not like ya'll were being quiet about it ma'am." Alexis looked down and paused for a second and he was right; the group she sat with for coffee had a tendency to get loud. "Can I steal ten minutes of your time? I assure ya, I ain't a freak or anything."

Looking at her watch, around the shop, then back at the man, she felt safe there with so many people that she knew and although part of her was cautious, the precocious part was too curious to let this go, so she said, "Sure." She sat back down. "What do you want to know?"

"Let's just say I'm on a committee of sorts, I can't really tell you any details."

"CIA? FBI?" She inquired as she continued to look directly into his eyes waiting for an answer.

"Part of my job is to search out pornography users and that's about all I can tell ya."

"So far we have established the fact that you are an eavesdropper, blunt and good at evading questions. So what can I do for you?" Alexis said sarcastically.

"Not reacting to her sarcasms in anyway, he asked, "How can ya tell just by lookin at a man if he's addicted to pornography?"

"I'm not sure I can explain it in ten minutes but one of my theories is you have to have known evil to be able to recognize evil. In other words, I was married to an evil man who was also addicted to pornography and it was not until after that experience that I realized I recognized the look."

"What does the look, look like?"

"It's hard to explain; I'd have to show you. It's recognizable from the side of the face as well as the front of the face but you have to be able to see the eyes. It used to freak me out but you would be surprised how many guys have the look. I am beginning to notice it in younger guys more than I ever use to as well as the older ones."

"This is just a theory though, right? I mean, ya never done any research or testin of your theory, so in a sense you are only speculatin."

"Second fact we have established is that you are direct in your questioning and arrogant." Alexis cocked her head a little to the left. "Are you a lawyer?"

"Arrogant? Lawyer?" He laughed. "Come now. Really, ya have no proof for yer claim little lady, so yer just speculatin right?"

"You can call it whatever you want Mr…."Alexis was hoping he would fill in the blank, and looked at him in question.

Once again, he ignored her. "Are ya able to teach me this look?"

"Why would you want to learn the look if you don't believe in the look?" Alexis was getting aggravated with him.

"I didn't say I didn't believe in it. I just wanted to establish the fact that it is just a hypothesis so far, however, if it will aid in my job, I am willing to consider it; maybe even to help prove it."

Alexis sat silent for a minute not knowing what to think of the man; she couldn't tell if she liked him a lot or hated him and it aggravated her all the more that she was intrigued by him…he was interested in proving her hypothesis?

"I don't know if I can teach you the look or not. I use to wonder if I had some sort of gift to be able to recognize it or if it was something that could be learned, but I have been trying to educate my sixteen year old daughter and have been pointing the look out to her. She seems to have picked up on what it looks like a little so it might be something that can be learned, I don't know. The first place I noticed it was in the man I was married to of course, but then if you look at every man in the paper arrested for sexual crimes, they all have the same look about their eyes. It's scary."

He looked at the paper on the table. "Here's a paper right here. Show me what yer talkin bout."

"You sure are different than anyone I've met around here." Alexis held her hand out over the table. "By the way, I am Alexis Cole."

"Sorry. I am Ben Wright." He shook her hand and sat down across the table from her.

Alexis chuckled sarcastically and shook her head. "Yeah and my cousin Done Wrong will be here shortly."

"Ya sure are a feisty one."

Alexis picked up the newspaper, found the local section and started to turn the pages. "Ok. Let's see if we have any sexual crimes in the paper today. Can't imagine us not having any with the way it has been lately. She found the one they were discussing earlier: Here we go…see that." She laid the paper down on the table and pointed to a fifty-two year old man that had been arrested for raping a seven year old girl. "That's the look you are looking for right there." Ben looked at the picture.

Right about then a young man walked into the coffee shop and Alexis noticed the look on him. Once he passed their table, she quietly told Ben about it. "Don't turn around now, but in a minute check out the guy in the blue t-shirt in line. He has the look. You can see it in person."

It was hard for Ben not to turn around immediately but in his line of work self control was of paramount importance and he had learned to have power over himself against natural tendencies when necessary. Eventually Ben was able to discreetly get a good look at the guy.

170

"Sometimes I feel like this is sinful." Alexis said as she looked down.

"What?" He asked her.

"Well, the Bible says that man looks at the outward appearance but God looks at the heart. I could be totally wrong about all of this…the look and all; speculations as you called it."

"The Bible also says, in His light we see light. Do you ever see that look?"

"All the time; it's the face of illumination because of the spirit of God within a person. Are you a Christian?" She was excitedly curious.

"Yep."

"No way!" Alexis said in sarcastic but protected relief.

"Yes ma'am, I am. Grew up in Texas; went to church three times a week."

"That makes me feel a little better about you. I've never discussed this topic with a total stranger; you're still different."

"Yeah, us Texans are a whole other breed." He studied her face. "The look of illumination; it's weird isn't it; ya meet someone ya know you've never met before and yet they seem familiar to ya."

Alexis looked at him forgetting about what they were supposed to be talking about now that she felt a slight bit more comfortable with him. She could not deny he was a good looking man in spite of being different and their eyes were locked as if looking away was out of their control. The mutual attraction was obvious but neither wanted the other to know. Finally, Alexis forced herself to look down. "So what's your story? Married? Divorced? How old are you anyway?" She was embarrassed that she had just blurted it all out.

He grinned and looked down at his feet and back up. "Honestly, Alexis, I can't answer any questions; I've told you too much already but it is a risk I am willing to take for the purpose at hand."

"And what purpose is that?"

He threw his hands up slightly. "Do you want me to lie to you? I could answer all your questions if all yer after is the satisfaction of havin yer questions answered or your expectations me. After all, isn't that what most people are after in life: getting their expectations met?"

He was an arrogant little cuss and his response drove her nuts. "You sure are mysterious in an annoying kind of way Mr. Ben Wright." This was the nicest way she could find to express her emotion. She took a sip of coffee, then made a face; it was cold.

Alexis allowed no admission of guilt for her opinion of him, good looking or not, even if he really was brethren; she wasn't even sure he was telling the truth about that. She was an information gatherer and had always been ever since she was a little girl. People who interrupted the flow of her "data input task" irritated her. But Ben had long ago quit apologizing for the requirements his job entailed. Either people accepted it or didn't; it was as simple as that and he knew that in time people always made their choice one way or the other.

172

It was obvious to her that he had some kind of formal training in psychology and although her mind desired the satisfaction of real answers to all her questions, she decided if she could not get the answers from him she was going to make them up from her own imagination. She purposed that he did in fact work for the CIA and was involved with a special mission of sorts; perhaps a task force with the goal of eradicating pornography, even though she considered this to be an impossible undertaking or maybe he was involved in a sting operation against the mob. Everyone knows they basically own the porn industry. Yes, she would choose a noble calling for him, since he was allowing her the assignment of such by mere lack of information. She also had decided he had been married before but had allowed his job to destroy the relationship and now he was mostly all business. Her mind wanted to believe that he was unattached.

Alexis surmised it was fun filling in the multiple choice answers about whom Ben was from her mind's list of possibilities. Her psyche wandered from place to place and landed on the exciting thought that they were attracted to each other; she smiled. He wasn't wearing a wedding ring and he was a Christian; if he was telling the truth that is. In her mind, she saw him…he was everything Kurt couldn't be: strong and stable…

"Have you ever visited a prison?" He asked her with no response so he tried a second time. "Alexis?"

Alexis suddenly realized he was talking to her and was startled, "Oh, I'm sorry. I was just thinking."

"About what?"

She quickly changed the subject to try to cover up where she had let her thoughts meander. "Have you ever seen Dr. Dobson's interview with Ted Bundy?"[6]

"No."

"That would be a great place for you to start. Ted Bundy had the look big time and there is a lot of good information in that interview."

Ben picked up his keys and looked at them. She noticed he was fiddling around with a little device on the key chain that looked like a bracelet charm but wasn't. She figured it was some kind of guy gadget.

"Anyone else in here you see with the look besides the guy in the blue t-shirt Miss Alex?"

"Alex?" She questioned. "My name is Alexis, thank you."

"No ma'am, to me yer Miss Alex…that's what fits."

"I'm not sure if I like you very much." Alexis hated being called Alex.

"That's quite all right; you don't have to like me. Since when did liking someone become criteria for getting a job done?"

He had a way of stumping her that she had not experienced with anyone else and he was very different than most guys she had been attracted to. He did not say all the right things and did not even act like he cared whether or not he said all the right things. Once again, he was right. She had complained in the past to her friends about her places of employment, that it seemed like people were there for a social club instead of performing a job and if they didn't like someone, they could not work with them, incapable of agreeing to disagree and move on in a professional manner still able to perform their responsibilities.

"We should probably be done for today; I gotta go." Alexis stood up and began gathering her things.

"Oh, so you are a flight individual."

"What?"

"A flight individual; most people are either a 'flight' or 'fight' when confronted."

Alexis rolled her eyes and put her purse on her shoulder. "By the way, the manager of this coffee shop has the look." She turned from him and walked out the door.

By the time her errands were done three hours later, she arrived home and found a small potted, brightly colored flower on her front door step. There was no note, although something told her it was from Ben. She began to feel creepy about him and embarrassed that she had been attracted to him.

"Why did I give him my real name; I'm such an idiot." She was talking out loud to herself as she brought things in the house from the car. "Wait a minute! If he's from the CIA he probably knows everything about me by now including my bra size and there is probably a recorder inside that plant. He probably recorded our whole conversation with that little device thingy he had on his keys. What if he is a terrorist and there is a bomb in the flower?" Alexis' voice was progressively getting louder.

175

"Mom, who are you talking to out here?" Her daughter asked coming out from her room.

"No one."

"Then why are you talking out loud?"

"Honestly, teenagers can be annoying." Alexis mumbled softly as she went to the front door, opened it, picked up the flower, brought it through the house to the back door and chucked it into the woods.

"What are you doing?" Her daughter asked in horror.

"Nothing."

"Mom, have you lost your mind? Why did you just throw my flower out into the woods?

Alexis stopped in her tracks as mortification made its way to her face. "What? That was your flower?"

"Yeah; 'was' being the optimum word."

"Oh, I'm so sorry…I didn't know." Alexis put her hand over her mouth.

"You could have asked." Her daughter walked into her room and slammed the door.

Alexis went to her daughter's bedroom door, knocked and slowly opened it speaking softly. "I'm really sorry. Let's run up to the store and I'll get you another flower. Where did you get that one?"

"A boy at school."

"Someone you like?"

"No, but I was going to plant it anyway. Why did you do that, I don't understand."

"I met this creepy guy at the coffee shop today and I got freaked out I guess. Come on, let's run up to the store and I'll tell you all about it. We'll stop and get barbeque for dinner." Alexis said in a teasing voice.

Her daughter agreed to go, pulled pork was her favorite and she couldn't resist. Alexis went over some of the details on the drive there.

"So what if this guy is some kind of weirdo?" Her daughter asked.

"I know, that's why I got freaked out and paranoid."

"That little device on his key chain is probably a camera mom."

"Nut uh."

"Duh."

The next day at the coffee shop Ben was there. Alexis thought about leaving but refused to allow him to invoke fear in her to the point of altering her behavior; that would mean she had given him control over her. This was her coffee spot, not his. With coffee and the usual power bagel in hand Alexis sat down with her friends. She couldn't help but look over at Ben at one point out of inquisitiveness and it was an awkward moment because he was looking at her. He nodded as if to say hello. She looked away. An hour went by quickly as the conversation at the table traveled from current event to current event and the pressure on her bladder told

177

her it was time to head to the ladies room. A portion of her friends decided to leave and she said good-bye before walking to the bathroom.

Once behind the closed locked door, she wondered about Ben…would he still be there when she came out? The button on the toilet did not work properly and hadn't worked properly for two years so when she was done she held it down as usual while the toilet flushed, washed her hands then headed out the door.

"Don't you ever work?"

Alexis jumped. "You scared me."

"Didn't mean to." Ben was standing in the dark hallway leading to the restrooms. "Can we talk? You were right."

"Right about what?" Alexis continued walking past him and toward the table where she had left her purse.

He followed her. "The look; all three men including the one in jail are addicted to pornography."

"How did you…"

"Miss Alex, please let's not go through this again; please don't make me disappoint ya by not being able to answer yer questions."

"But how am I supposed to communicate with you or have a conversation? I don't like one sided relationships; I've had enough of them to last a life time."

"I know."

"See…like that! WHAT do you know? I'm not sure I can handle not knowing what you know about me that I don't know you know. There's a concrete wall around you fifty feet high and yet I stand in front of you buck naked."

Alexis walked back to the table and said, "Great!" out loud, when she got there. She had not taken her purse to the restroom and everyone at the table was gone, and now her purse was missing. "Great friends!" She turned around to see Ben standing there holding her purse out to her; she grabbed it from him and said thank you. He was unaffected by her noticeable disconcertion.

"I did some research last night."

"Oh yeah?" Alexis said uninterested as she got her keys out of her purse.

"Where are you going?"

"Ben, I'm freaked out about you. You are a total, complete stranger to me and I don't feel comfortable with any of this, especially since you have to be so secretive about whom you really are. I have enough trouble keeping up with reality never mind superficiality." Alexis' voice was louder than normal.

"Why do you run from that which you shouldn't and embrace that which you should run from?"

"What?"

"I understand if ya have to go Miss Alex, that would be a perfectly normal reaction to what ya have experienced with me so far, but I really think yer are on to something with this gift ya have to see this look or whatever it is ya see in people and I need ya. I need ya to help me."

"I can't do this right now…I need time to think ok?" With this she turned and walked out the door to her car.

CHAPTER EIGHT

"Hi. This is Alexis Cole. Can I please make an appointment with Dr. Billings for this week if he has any openings." Alexis was hoping she could touch base just to make sure she wasn't loosing her mind about Ben, and tell Dr. Billings about the dreams she had the night after she met him; maybe he could explain them to her.

"Actually, Ms. Cole, we just had a cancellation for tomorrow…can you make it at five thirty?" The voice asked on the other line.

"That'd be great. See ya then, five thirty."

Alexis loved Dr. Billings' lobby, it felt so comforting and safe. The music playing on the overhead speakers was not like the loud and obnoxious muzak playing in most public venues, but was acoustical and calming…and they were singing about God. However, the last time she had been in the lobby was almost two years ago and it brought back a distaste that made her shake her head again about the whole relationship with Kurt and she was grieved over how much of her life she had wasted with him, then tried to drown that thought by how God had used it for good. She abandoned her thoughts as Dr. Billings came in the room.

"Come in Alexis. Good to see you." Dr. Billings was a tall individual with a voice that avoided emotion in order to have a soothing affect on others which is the way it always happened with Alexis any time she heard him speak.

"Hi. How have you been?" Alexis asked as she walked into the room. Dr. Billings thoughtfully chose a different room than the one Alexis was so familiar with.

"Good. Had more surgery on the eye, but it is fine now. What brings you here today?"

"I just wanted to touch base with you. I met this guy and it has been weird to say the least. We're not dating...I mean, he's just an acquaintance at this point, but I want to understand some of what I am feeling about him, or what I'm feeling about why I don't like the way I'm feeling."

"Explain." He said without any emotional reaction and with a complete monotone in his voice.

"Ok...He approached me at the coffee shop a few days ago because he overheard a conversation I was having and he asked me a question about it."

"He was listening?" Dr. Billings asked.

"Yeah, but we were being very loud and he wasn't very far away." Alexis guessed what he was thinking.

"Ok."

"Well, I tried to talk to him and while he is an extremely attractive man, it just seemed like I was skinning the palms of my hands on payment."

"The conversation went that well?"

"Yeah!" Alexis laughed. "He frustrated me so much and I don't know why, but then at the same time I am attracted to him. I don't understand this at all and I want to make sure he is not that

182

type of guy you told me about that I would continue to attract. I want to do preventative maintenance sort to speak."

"Good thinking. Has he asked you out?"

"No."

"Do you think he approached you in hopes of any romantic interest? Did he seem interested in you?"

"No. He approached me because of his work but it does kind of seem like we are attracted to each other."

"How long have you known him?"

"A few days." Alexis began to feel ridiculous for being there but knew if she was going to break patterns in her life, she needed outside help for the things she couldn't see for herself and not after the fact but before. So she went on to tell Dr. Billings more of what happened that day at the bagel shop.

"What exactly was it about him that frustrated you?"

"Well, he couldn't answer any of my questions."

"Why?"

"He's some kind of undercover person on an undercover mission and he can't tell me much about himself."

"Why would it frustrate you not to have this information?"

"Because I want to know."

"For what purpose? What will you do with the information?"

"Decide."

"Decide what?"

"I guess, decide if I like him or not." Dr. Billings had a way of getting people to go through the mental pathways that led them to their own conclusions. "

"Maybe you have an unhealthy desire to sum people up too quickly. Why would it be important for you to decide so quickly whether you like him or not?"

"Because..." Alexis hesitated. "I don't know. He is very different than any guy I've ever been attracted to before. I had this dream and I think it is all related somehow…maybe that is what is causing my confusion."

"Tell me about it."

Alexis closed her eyes. "There were horses, lots of them, running around, seemingly disorganized, but not frightful. It wasn't like I was trying to catch one, or find one, I was just watching them and standing there; they could see me. A particular horse found me; it seemed to have picked me out, came over to me and encouraged me by nuzzling my arm to stroke its mane and coat, so I did."

"Did you want to?"

"Oh yeah!" Alexis answered enthusiastically. "It was a fine-looking horse and it made me happy that it was the only one that approached me. I was surprised by it coming over to me, I was not expecting it. It was a beautiful horse with a tan coat, white socks, a white star on its head and a cream colored mane. Eventually it invited me and allowed me to put my arms around its neck and be affectionate toward it nuzzling me the whole time. It was different from the rest, more striking, then it had to go somewhere but gave me the impression that it would be back. At this point I woke up, but then I drifted back to sleep and began dreaming again."

"When did this dream occur?"

Alexis opened her eyes and looked at Dr. Billings. "The night I met Ben. That is his name, Ben."

Dr. Billings was writing on his pad of paper. "Ok, continue."

"So immediately following the horse dream I had another dream. I was free falling dressed in a white covering like a choir robe from very high up but I was safe not scared. I was hesitant to fall but then was assured by something. There was a song playing in the background; I knew the song very well and smiled. I could hear the words very clearly. It's a song I know from the radio that basically is a guy encouraging a woman to fall and he says he will catch her."[7]

"Interesting." Dr. Billings picked up his dream books that had been referenced back when Alexis had so many spiritual dreams during her ordeal with Kurt. He read what certain words meant and deciphered the dream for Alexis.

"You're not really helping me at all. It's almost like you are encouraging me to run to Ben.

"Well, I don't know if I would go that far. Did you want me to tell you to run away from him as fast as you could?"

"That certainly would have been easier."

"From what you are telling me, he sounds like the complete opposite of the guys you have attracted in the past and I don't think you should run away, but just get to know him slowly. The fact that

185

he did not get upset when you got upset, and that he was not afraid to show emotion around you, like when he threw his hands up in the air, proves that he is very different than the guys you have typically attracted and comfortable with who he is from the beginning. The guys you typically have attracted act perfect from the beginning because they are afraid to show emotion or experience anything unpleasant, they are afraid of their own skin and don't even know who they are, trying to get you to believe they are perfect. This guy seems to not care if you think he is perfect or not. Remember, it takes time to really get to know someone so don't worry about too much too soon, just go slow. Time always has a way of revealing truth remember?"

"Yeah, I remember."

"If he is in fact the opposite of the guys you have attracted in the past, that means he is more like you, so just be careful and make sure you appreciate him for those things in yourself that you like. Let him be him, and you be you. It is harder at first when two people are alike but becomes easier with time, and typically if people are opposites it gets harder as time goes on and seems like a dream come true in the beginning. A suggestion to you…"

"Yeah?"

"Calm down. You don't even know yet if this guy is ever going to ask you out or be interested in you in a romantic way."

Alexis knew Dr. Billings was right and as she drove away from the appointment she felt better about Ben and confident knowing that the truth would in fact reveal itself eventually if she

186

just gave it enough time. She acknowledged that she had a tendency to be very impatient, and project too far into the future with what-ifs, so she planned on working to change that and calming down as Dr. Billings had put it. She also knew that she had been out of the romantic loop for awhile and being nervous was normal. In essence, after talking with Dr. Billings she felt relieved and not fearful she would run into Ben again at the coffee shop.

If almost predictable, Ben was having coffee the next morning when Alexis walked in to the bagel shop. This day was different than the other days she had seen Ben because today she was dressed for work; the first time he had ever seen her fixed up or in professional clothing; an off white jacket, matching straight skirt four inches above the knee, light blue lacey camisole underneath, cream colored heels and hair down and around her face. In the past, when he had seen her, she had the day off and was dressed very casually with her hair up. As she looked at him while she walked to the end of the counter to order her bagel, he did a double take when he saw her and just about spilled his coffee. She chuckled and turned to the attendant. Now she knew for sure he was in fact attracted to her and he was still staring at her when she looked at him again minutes after ordering her food.

Maybe it was because of the appointment with Dr. Billings and her new confidence about dealing with Ben, or maybe it was because she was just too tired of the games people play to worry about it any longer, whatever the reason, Alexis walked over to Ben as if he had never frustrated her before and held her hand out.

"Good morning to you Mr. Ben Wright." She said his name in a tone that made him know that she knew that was not his real name.

He shook her hand. "Good mornin. Ya look nice."

"Thank you. Just wanted to say hi; I gotta run…work."

"Have a good day." He said as she started walking away. "Hey, when can we get together and talk?"

"Don't know." She responded as she headed out the door never looking back at him. "That was fun." She said quietly out loud and smiled.

Later that day at work she checked her emails. There was one from a name she did not recognize, but spam guard had not sent it to the spam file, so she opened it. The file was a beautiful red rose bud that opened within seconds before her eyes. Once the rose finished opening, there was a message inside of it…it said, "Call me as soon as you get this message, Ben", and it listed a phone number. It sounded urgent and so she called the number.

"Hello. How are ya Miss Alex?"

"I'm fine Ben. Is everything ok?"

"Yes, why do ya ask?"

"Your message sounded urgent."

"How could it have sounded urgent; I wasn't speaking audibly?"

"Typically, 'as soon as you can', means there is something urgent."

"To my knowledge, 'as soon as ya can', means as soon as ya can, instead of later than ya can." Ben laughed.

"You think you're funny don't you?" Alexis said in a playful but frustrated voice.

"Women! Always jumpin to conclusions."

"Men! Thinking they're always right."

"Ok, well now that we've gotten that out of the way…do ya have any time tonight?"

"For what?" Alexis was very curious and amazed at how he had just transitioned her thoughts from one place to another.

"I'd like to take ya to dinner."

Alexis caught her breath, then hesitated and thought about how she really did not even know this person. For all she knew, he could be lying about everything he had told her all the way down to where he grew up. A myriad of feelings ran through her…dinner? The thought of having dinner across the table from a guy she was highly attracted to, was an enjoyable thought to say the least.

"Miss Alex?"

"Oh, sorry. Uhmm…yes, I think I am free tonight. Where shall I meet you?" She could not believe what she was saying.

"I'll come pick ya up. How is seven?"

"That'd be fine. You know where I live?"

"Yes, ma'am, I do."

"You probably know a lot more than that."

He ignored her. "I'll see ya bout seven."

"Ok."

Alexis hung up the phone, various thoughts making their way through the pathways of her mind until she was mentally exhausted and sick of thinking. She grabbed a stack of papers and continued working on the project she started earlier that day; it needed to be done by tomorrow.

That night, Ben picked her up for dinner at five minutes after seven. The conversation was easy and quickly turned flirty. Occasionally, as they walked into the restaurant, his hand would brush up against hers. They laughed and shared stories of their childhoods, but did not talk about "the look" at all, not once. She had been attracted to him before, but now it was moving toward a desire to be closer, to touch him.

After dinner, they decided to drive to the beach a few miles away, and take a walk. It was a full moon tonight and the moon's reflection on the ocean was bright and beautiful, the shore lit up as if someone knew they would be there at that particular time and had created a perfect romantic setting. A soft breeze had come in from the northwest and it made the air comfortable and less humid. The waves crashed to the sand, the sound of forced ocean slapping down onto the ground loud enough to be heard but comforting enough not to interfere with the conversation.

Typically Alexis never walked on the beach at night; it was just not safe, especially for a woman, alone. However, here, next to Ben, there was no question in her mind that she was safe and protected and would not end up in the newspaper the next day as a statistic. Ben gave the appearance of being able to defend a woman by the simple beauty of his build that refused to be hidden by his clothes; although it was obvious he did not try to flaunt his body.

They did not walk far from the boardwalk and stood there on the shore watching the waves. Momentary stretches of silence were not uncomfortable and just seemed to substantiate the fact they felt relaxed together tonight. At one point, he placed his hand up under her hair line at the back of her neck gently and leaned in to kiss her. She turned and began walking away slowly talking about how nice dinner was and that she needed to get up early in the morning, surprised by her own reaction to his electric touch.

"Ben, I think we should go. I've got an early appointment with a client tomorrow." Although she really did have an appointment in the morning, Alexis was using this as an excuse to escape because she was suddenly uncomfortable but didn't know why.

"It has been a fun and relaxin evenin…I needed this. Thank ya." Ben felt her discomfort. He knew more about her than she realized and he understood, so he did not let it bother him or counter react to her at all.

"Yes, I enjoyed it too."

With that said, Ben held his hand out in the direction of the boardwalk as if to point and say, shall we walk back? There was not much talking on the drive to Alexis' house and Ben could tell that she was deep in thought so he didn't interrupt. He dropped her off at her house, walked her to the front door, and said good night without an attempted kiss.

As the front door closed, Alexis took a deep breath and sighed in relief. There was something that just did not feel right to her about Ben. Maybe it was the lack of detailed information about him; maybe it was just her. Whatever the case, her instinct was telling her not to get attached right now. This confused her because she knew in the past she thought she was right when she discerned Kurt, however, she had been one hundred percent wrong; trying to figure other people out was arduous.

She began talking out loud to herself, "I know why I haven't dated; this is annoying, not being able to see into someone's heart; not being able to know what they are thinking, or if they are just after whatever they can get, or really interested in me as a person." She started to pray: "Dear Lord, God you've been there with me the whole time. You know my every thought, my every desire, you made me. You know my rising and my laying down, you know my coming and my going. The feelings deep within me as a woman, you created and placed inside of me. The desire to be loved and love back. The desire to be wanted. God I know that it is you and you alone who has my best interest in mind perfectly. You never fail or make a mistake. Please reveal to me why I am feeling that something is not right about Ben. Please protect me from evil. I covet your blessings. In Christ's name, Amen." Praying always made Alexis feel better and seemed to calm her spirit making it possible for her to lay down and get a good night's sleep.

The next morning when Alexis heard the phone ringing, she thought she was dreaming. "Hello."

"Good morning, Alex."

She recognized the voice. "Hi Ben. What time is it?"

"About six-thirty."

"What's up?"

"Can you meet me at the coffee shop today for lunch?"

"Uhmm, I think so; everything all right?"

"Yes, everything is fine. See ya bout noon-ish?"

"That works."

Alexis hung up the phone and stumbled into the shower. She wondered what it was that Ben had to talk to her about, or did he just want to see her? So when it came time to meet, she was early. As he walked toward the coffee shop she observed him, walking confidently and carrying himself professionally. He looked very good and she felt silly for becoming uncomfortable with him last night and in a way wished that she had let him kiss her, curious about whether or not it would have been as magnificent as she had imagined it would have been. But a voice inside her head reminded her that even if it had been the most extraordinary kiss she ever experienced that that was no guarantee for a great relationship.

"Hey, good morning." Ben said as he took her hand and gave her a courteous side kiss which surprised her; he had never done that before.

They ordered the broiled chicken bagel lunch meal, got some coffee and sat down.

"So did you have something you needed to tell me?"

"I need to ask you to do something for me, for work."

"Oh boy, I can't wait to hear this. Before you do that though, I want to apologize for last night."

"What about last night?"

"I became uncomfortable with you and kind of cut things short, sorry. My emotions get whacked sometimes as a woman."

"Don't worry about it."

"Thank you."

Ben brought the conversation back to where he had started it a minute ago.

"What I need you to do is risky."

"I don't like risk. Maybe you are asking the wrong person."

"With your knowledge of men, you are perfect for the job."

"I'm not sure that's a compliment." Alexis studied his face.

"I need you to join the gym down the street and make friends with this guy, enough to get him to ask you out."

"Are you crazy?" Alexis couldn't believe what she was hearing and her tone of voice was the clue.

"No. Not crazy at all. I just need to get into this guy's apartment."

"Surely you can do that without me?"

"I need you to be in the apartment with him, distracting him, so I can come in when the alarm system has been turned off."

"Can't a guy like you deactivate the alarm system?"

"Not this one."

"You're absolutely nuts. I've come to that conclusion, if I know nothing else about you."

"Ok, how much money would it take for you to help me?"

"What?"

"I said how much money would it take for you to help me?"

"I know what you said, but I don't understand. You would pay me to help you?"

"Well, not me personally."

"Oh yeah, the so called people you work for."

"Five thousand? Would you do it for five thousand?"

"You're gonna pay me five thousand dollars to meet some guy at a gym, get him to ask me out, then go back to his apartment with him? What if he expects me to sleep with him?"

"He won't. He's gay."

"What?" Alexis' surprised response was loud and caused other patrons to look at her. Her body language indicated that at any moment she was going to get up and leave.

"He uses women as a cover up. I can't tell ya too much because I don't want to ruin this effort, but I have been trying to get him for a long time. He runs a huge child pornography ring but uses women as a cover up. He'll get you in his apartment, make ya lay on his sofa or bed, lay next to ya, kiss your cheek, and take pictures of it so that he has photos to put on his website and show people at his work that make him seem like a normal red blooded American guy."

"Ew. Will you ever stop giving me the creeps?"

"Probably not. I need to get in and do something with his computer. So you would need to inadvertently leave the door unlocked and get him outside to his balcony for awhile."

"I don't know about all of this." Alexis' head was swimming.

"Ten thousand?"

"Why don't you just act gay and get him to ask you out?"

"Very funny. He doesn't like men, only boys and if I'm making out with him on the balcony how can I get what I need from the computer."

"Ew, ew and double ew."

"Fifteen thousand?"

"Ben, you're crazy. Do you expect me to give you an answer right now? I mean, No. No is the answer, I don't care how much money you offer me."

"I do need to know you answer soon; time is of the essence. Twenty thousand is my last offer. If you won't do it, then I have to find someone else."

"I already told you No."

"I'm not accepting that as an answer. Think about it ok?"

Alexis heard Ben's i-phone ring and looked down onto the table where he had placed it after reading an email. Before he could pick it up, she saw the reminder, "1 p.m. wedding anniversary".

"Wedding anniversary? Are you married?" She asked in a tone of voice that sounded like, "it figures".

"I've got to get going. I will call you in a little while to get your answer ok?" Ben said as he went out the door without an answer to the married question.

"Whatever." Alexis said after he was already out of ear shot.

Uncertainties ran through her mind collecting particles of disappointment as they traveled all the way to her heart. She had not realized an emotional attachment had happened with Ben and was not quite sure what to do about it.

One of the clerk's at the bagel shop that Alexis had known for years and was close to, walked over to her.

"Can I talk to you for a minute?"

Alexis looked at him, he typically wasn't this serious. "Sure, have a seat."

"You know, I get some strange vibes from that guy you meet in here for coffee."

"You do?"

"Yeah, I do. Do you know him very well?"

"No, I don't know much about him at all."

"I've got a funny feeling about it, but I think you should stay away from him."

"Sure, you're just saying that so you can get close to me."

They both laughed.

"No, seriously. I just got a feeling about it and I had to share it with you even though it is none of my business."

Alexis looked down and shook her head. "There is something strange about him isn't there?"

"Sorry."

"It's ok. Thanks for your concern. It doesn't do anything at all to help me with the funny vibes I was getting about him though, except confirm that maybe I am right, but thanks for the info." The gentleman stood up and walked back behind the coffee counter and Alexis left.

The next morning cloudless sky was the back drop for the sunrise as Alexis sat alone on the wooden walkway railing watching. It always amazed her how bright and orange that big ball shown and how it made anything in her life that seemed disorganized and frustrating seem so small and inconsequential. Coming to nature of any kind grounded Alexis; brought her back to reality front and center; realigned her priorities. It was here at the beach, close enough to the ocean to touch it whenever she wanted, that decisions were made, prayers prayed, memories filed, emotions categorized and brought into subjection, costs counted, thoughts accepted or rejected, boundaries settled on, and raw truth allowed to flow until answers emerged forth. So when her mind decided that it was time to end the madness of knowing Ben, it all made perfect sense to her without doubt or question, the salt air seemingly eroding away any would-be vacillation. Brown pelicans flying in "V" formation high above her, their beauty of gliding through the air effortlessly confirmed her thoughts that a relationship with Ben, even if just as friends, was too wearisome for her, too exhausting and laborious, before it even started. It felt good to purge the attachment she had made, to surrender to her spiritual instincts, and that gut feeling that something just wasn't right about him or right about her getting involved with him.

There are opportunities in life when emotions afford us the courage to do the right thing and when those occasions are not fully taken advantage of, wrong paths are traveled down, paving scars into the hearts of many. Alexis couldn't wait for the time when all truth would be revealed and there was nothing more to figure out, nothing more to guess about intentions and motives of other people; a place where all was transparent and beautiful, a place where deception didn't exist. Where there are no tears or sorrow, no pain. She knew it was part of her burden to bear on this earth being subjected to all these things, but looked forward to the time they would be eliminated. It was when she sat quietly and observed creation for an extended period of time that Alexis felt closest to her God, closest to his promises. His creation was an open letter to all who would read it, a guarantee of his power, and a display of His might.

Footnotes:

[1] Nathaniel Hawthorne - Scarlet Letter – public domain
[2] Ulysses S. Grant quote – public domain
[3] Alexis did not realize until after she discovered the NPD info that the reason Kurt did this was because earlier at the baseball fields, Alexis had been speaking with one of the coaches who was extremely good looking, and it made Kurt jealous although he did

not give any hint that he was jealous or say anything about it. That would be facing reality; something he was incapable of. Therefore, he created a scene in which he knew she would get jealous, so he could channel his jealousy through her. He projected his negative feelings onto her for her to experience for him so he did not have to, for he was incapable of doing it for himself because that would be real. This was his way of subconsciously circumventing the pain of reality that he had never been taught to process.

[4] Steve Bell CD entitled: Beyond A Shadow – song entitled, "Burning Ember".

Permission granted by Steve Bell via facebook message.

[5] Truly the best information out there regarding the subject of Narcissistic Personality Disorder is a book by Sam Vaknin entitled, Malignant Self Love.

Permission granted by Sam Vaknin vie email.

[6] Dr. James Dobson interview of Ted Bundy. Permission granted.

[7] Song written by Clay Mills entitled "Fall". Permission granted.

Manufactured by Amazon.ca
Bolton, ON

13892496R00118